SECOND EDITION

ALL ABOUT THE USA 2

A Cultural Reader

Milada Broukal
Peter Murphy

PEARSON
Longman

All About the USA 2: A Cultural Reader, Second Edition

Pearson Education, 10 Bank Street, White Plains, NY 10606

Staff credits: The people who made up the *All About the USA* team, representing editorial, production, design, and manufacturing, are: Wendy Campbell, Nan Clarke, Dave Dickey, Dana Klinek, Laura LeDréan, Melissa Leyva, Michael Mone, Rob Ruvo, Keyana Shaw.

Cover art: Pat Wosczyk

Photo credits: **p. 1** © MAPS.com/Corbis; **p. 5** © Raymond Gehman/Corbis; **p. 9** © Bargas Henry/Corbis Sygma; **p. 13** © Bettmann/Corbis; **p. 18** © Lee Snider/Photo Images/Corbis; **p. 23** © Bettmann/Corbis; **p. 27** © Tim Shaffer/Reuters/Corbis; **p. 32** © Corbis; **p. 37** (top left) Bill Brooks/Alamy, (top right) Jon Arnold Images/Alamy, (bottom left) Dennis Hallinan/Alamy, (bottom right) © Lee Snider Photo Images/Corbis; **p. 41** Lisa F. Young/Fotolia; **p. 45** © Prisma RM/Glow Images; **p. 49** Clipart.com/© Jupiterimages Corporation; **p. 54** © Bettmann/Corbis; **p. 59** colinspics/Alamy; **p. 64** © Bettmann/Corbis; **p. 69** © Kelly-Mooney Photography/Corbis; **p. 74** North Wind Picture Archives/Alamy; **p. 79** © Bettmann/Corbis; **p. 84** © Reuters/Corbis; **p. 89** © Bettmann/Corbis; **p. 94** © Alan Schein Photography/Corbis; **p. 99** Dawn Villella/ Associated Press; **p. 104** © Bettmann/Corbis; **p. 109** © Bettmann/Corbis; **p. 113** © Robert Galbraith/Reuters/Corbis; **p. 118** © Charles O'Rear/Corbis; **p. 123** © Joseph Sohm/Visions of America/Corbis; **p. 128** © Alan Schein/zefa/Corbis.

Text composition: Integra

Text font: 12/15 New Aster

Library of Congress Cataloging-in-Publication Data
Broukal, Milada.
  All about the USA / Milada Broukal.— 2nd ed.
    p. cm.
  Rev. ed. of: All about the USA, 1st ed. 1999.
  Revised ed. will be published in 4 separate volume levels.
  ISBN 0-13-613892-6 (student bk. with audio cd v. 1, : alk. paper)
  ISBN 0-13-240628-4 (student bk. with audio cd v. 2, : alk. paper)
  ISBN 0-13-234969-8 (student bk. with audio cd v. 3, : alk. paper)
  ISBN 0-13-234968-X (student bk. with audio cd v. 4, : alk. paper)
  1. Readers—United States. 2. English language—Textbooks for foreign speakers. 3. United States—Civilization—Problems, exercises, etc.
  I. Murphy, Peter (Peter Lewis Keane), 1947- II. Milhomme, Janet.
  III. Title.
  PE1127.H5B68 2008
  428.64—dc22

2007032614

ISBN-10: 0-13-240628-4
ISBN-13: 978-0-13-240628-4

Printed in the United States of America
7 8 9 10—V011—16 15 14 13

CONTENTS

INTRODUCTION

All About the USA 2 is a beginning reader for English language students. Twenty-eight units introduce typical American people, places, and things, providing students with essential information about the USA and stimulating cross-cultural exchange. The vocabulary and structures used in the text have been carefully controlled to help students gain fluency and confidence.

Each unit contains:
- An opening photo and prereading questions
- A short reading passage
- Topic-related vocabulary work
- Comprehension of main ideas
- Comprehension of details
- Discussion questions
- A writing activity
- *A Did You Know...?* section offering a fun fact about the topic

The **PREREADING** questions are linked to the photo on the first page of each unit. They focus the students on the topic of the unit by introducing names, encouraging speculation about content, involving the students' own experiences when possible, and presenting vocabulary as the need arises.

The **READING** passage for each unit ranges from about 200 to about 250 words. Students should first skim the passage for a general idea of the content. The teacher may wish to deal with some of the vocabulary at this point. The students should then read the passage carefully as they listen to the audio CD. Listening while reading helps students to comprehend and retain information in the reading.

The two **VOCABULARY** exercises focus on the boldfaced words in the reading. *Meaning*, a definition exercise, encourages students to work out the meanings of the target words from the context. Within this group are collocations, or groups of words that are easier to learn together. The second exercise, *Use*, reinforces the vocabulary further by making students use the words in a meaningful, yet possibly different, context. This section can be done during or after the reading phase, or both.

There are two **COMPREHENSION** exercises. *Looking for Main Ideas* should be used in conjunction with the text to help students develop reading skills, and not as a test of memory. Students are asked to confirm the basic content of the text, which they can do individually, in pairs, in small groups, or as a whole class. *Looking for Details* expands the students' exploration of the text, concentrating on the scanning skills necessary to derive maximum value from reading.

The **DISCUSSION** section gives the students the opportunity to bring their knowledge and imagination to the topics and related areas. They can discuss the questions with a partner or in small groups. The teacher may ask students to report back to the class on a given question.

The **WRITING** section prompts students to write simple sentences about a subject related to the topic of the unit. Teachers should use their own judgment when deciding whether to correct the writing exercises.

CONTENTS

INTRODUCTION

All About the USA 2 is a beginning reader for English language students. Twenty-eight units introduce typical American people, places, and things, providing students with essential information about the USA and stimulating cross-cultural exchange. The vocabulary and structures used in the text have been carefully controlled to help students gain fluency and confidence.

Each unit contains:
- An opening photo and prereading questions
- A short reading passage
- Topic-related vocabulary work
- Comprehension of main ideas
- Comprehension of details
- Discussion questions
- A writing activity
- *A Did You Know...?* section offering a fun fact about the topic

The **PREREADING** questions are linked to the photo on the first page of each unit. They focus the students on the topic of the unit by introducing names, encouraging speculation about content, involving the students' own experiences when possible, and presenting vocabulary as the need arises.

The **READING** passage for each unit ranges from about 200 to about 250 words. Students should first skim the passage for a general idea of the content. The teacher may wish to deal with some of the vocabulary at this point. The students should then read the passage carefully as they listen to the audio CD. Listening while reading helps students to comprehend and retain information in the reading.

The two **VOCABULARY** exercises focus on the boldfaced words in the reading. *Meaning*, a definition exercise, encourages students to work out the meanings of the target words from the context. Within this group are collocations, or groups of words that are easier to learn together. The second exercise, *Use*, reinforces the vocabulary further by making students use the words in a meaningful, yet possibly different, context. This section can be done during or after the reading phase, or both.

There are two **COMPREHENSION** exercises. *Looking for Main Ideas* should be used in conjunction with the text to help students develop reading skills, and not as a test of memory. Students are asked to confirm the basic content of the text, which they can do individually, in pairs, in small groups, or as a whole class. *Looking for Details* expands the students' exploration of the text, concentrating on the scanning skills necessary to derive maximum value from reading.

The **DISCUSSION** section gives the students the opportunity to bring their knowledge and imagination to the topics and related areas. They can discuss the questions with a partner or in small groups. The teacher may ask students to report back to the class on a given question.

The **WRITING** section prompts students to write simple sentences about a subject related to the topic of the unit. Teachers should use their own judgment when deciding whether to correct the writing exercises.

CONTENTS

INTRODUCTION

All About the USA 2 is a beginning reader for English language students. Twenty-eight units introduce typical American people, places, and things, providing students with essential information about the USA and stimulating cross-cultural exchange. The vocabulary and structures used in the text have been carefully controlled to help students gain fluency and confidence.

Each unit contains:
- An opening photo and prereading questions
- A short reading passage
- Topic-related vocabulary work
- Comprehension of main ideas
- Comprehension of details
- Discussion questions
- A writing activity
- *A Did You Know...?* section offering a fun fact about the topic

The **PREREADING** questions are linked to the photo on the first page of each unit. They focus the students on the topic of the unit by introducing names, encouraging speculation about content, involving the students' own experiences when possible, and presenting vocabulary as the need arises.

The **READING** passage for each unit ranges from about 200 to about 250 words. Students should first skim the passage for a general idea of the content. The teacher may wish to deal with some of the vocabulary at this point. The students should then read the passage carefully as they listen to the audio CD. Listening while reading helps students to comprehend and retain information in the reading.

The two **VOCABULARY** exercises focus on the boldfaced words in the reading. *Meaning*, a definition exercise, encourages students to work out the meanings of the target words from the context. Within this group are collocations, or groups of words that are easier to learn together. The second exercise, *Use*, reinforces the vocabulary further by making students use the words in a meaningful, yet possibly different, context. This section can be done during or after the reading phase, or both.

There are two **COMPREHENSION** exercises. *Looking for Main Ideas* should be used in conjunction with the text to help students develop reading skills, and not as a test of memory. Students are asked to confirm the basic content of the text, which they can do individually, in pairs, in small groups, or as a whole class. *Looking for Details* expands the students' exploration of the text, concentrating on the scanning skills necessary to derive maximum value from reading.

The **DISCUSSION** section gives the students the opportunity to bring their knowledge and imagination to the topics and related areas. They can discuss the questions with a partner or in small groups. The teacher may ask students to report back to the class on a given question.

The **WRITING** section prompts students to write simple sentences about a subject related to the topic of the unit. Teachers should use their own judgment when deciding whether to correct the writing exercises.

CONTENTS

INTRODUCTION

All About the USA 2 is a beginning reader for English language students. Twenty-eight units introduce typical American people, places, and things, providing students with essential information about the USA and stimulating cross-cultural exchange. The vocabulary and structures used in the text have been carefully controlled to help students gain fluency and confidence.

Each unit contains:
- An opening photo and prereading questions
- A short reading passage
- Topic-related vocabulary work
- Comprehension of main ideas
- Comprehension of details
- Discussion questions
- A writing activity
- *A Did You Know...?* section offering a fun fact about the topic

The **PREREADING** questions are linked to the photo on the first page of each unit. They focus the students on the topic of the unit by introducing names, encouraging speculation about content, involving the students' own experiences when possible, and presenting vocabulary as the need arises.

The **READING** passage for each unit ranges from about 200 to about 250 words. Students should first skim the passage for a general idea of the content. The teacher may wish to deal with some of the vocabulary at this point. The students should then read the passage carefully as they listen to the audio CD. Listening while reading helps students to comprehend and retain information in the reading.

The two **VOCABULARY** exercises focus on the boldfaced words in the reading. *Meaning*, a definition exercise, encourages students to work out the meanings of the target words from the context. Within this group are collocations, or groups of words that are easier to learn together. The second exercise, *Use*, reinforces the vocabulary further by making students use the words in a meaningful, yet possibly different, context. This section can be done during or after the reading phase, or both.

There are two **COMPREHENSION** exercises. *Looking for Main Ideas* should be used in conjunction with the text to help students develop reading skills, and not as a test of memory. Students are asked to confirm the basic content of the text, which they can do individually, in pairs, in small groups, or as a whole class. *Looking for Details* expands the students' exploration of the text, concentrating on the scanning skills necessary to derive maximum value from reading.

The **DISCUSSION** section gives the students the opportunity to bring their knowledge and imagination to the topics and related areas. They can discuss the questions with a partner or in small groups. The teacher may ask students to report back to the class on a given question.

The **WRITING** section prompts students to write simple sentences about a subject related to the topic of the unit. Teachers should use their own judgment when deciding whether to correct the writing exercises.

The Fifty States

PREREADING

Answer the questions.

1. What states can you name?
2. Where are they on the map?

The Fifty States

The fifty states of the United States, or the USA, make one **nation**. The United States did not always have fifty states. At first there were thirteen. As the United States grew, more states joined the union. The last two states to **join** were Alaska and Hawaii. They both joined in 1959.

The area of the United States covers every type of land. There are forests, deserts, mountains, and **flat land**. The area of the United States also covers every type of **climate**. The size of each state is different, too. Alaska is the biggest state. Rhode Island is the smallest state. Alaska is 500 times bigger than Rhode Island.

About 300 million people live in the United States. The people of the United States come from all over the world. People often named cities after where they came from. For example, in the United States you find Paris, Rome, Delhi, and Frankfurt. The state with the highest **population** is California. The state with the lowest population is Alaska.

Each state has its own name. The name gives the state its **identity** and personality. More than half the states have names of Native American **origin**. Each state also has a flag with colors that have a special meaning for the state. The flag is the **symbol of** the state. There is also a state flower, tree, and bird.

VOCABULARY

 MEANING

Complete the sentences with words from the box.

nation	flat land	population	origin
join	climate	identity	symbol of

1. Land that is level and not high is _____.

2. The beginning, or the point something starts from, is its _____.

3. The general weather at a particular place is the _____.

4. A group of states joined together is a _____.

5. A _____ something is a sign for it.

6. The number of people who live in one place is the _____.

7. You become part of something when you _____.

8. _____ tells us who someone or what something is.

USE

Work with a partner to answer the questions. Use complete sentences.

1. What is the *climate* like in the country you are living in?

2. What is the *population* of the country?

3. What is the *symbol* of a country or company you know?

4. What is the *origin* of your family?

5. What is the name of a *nation* you know?

6. What do you have to show your *identity*?

COMPREHENSION

LOOKING FOR MAIN IDEAS

Circle the letter of the best answer.

1. The United States _____ .
   a. was always fifty states
   b. has fifty states today
   c. is not a nation of fifty states

2. The United States has _____ .
   a. about 300 million people
   b. people from Europe and India only
   c. the highest population in the world

3. Each state has _____ .
   a. a Native American name
   b. no personality
   c. its own name and flag

One word in each sentence is *not* correct. Cross out the word and write the correct answer above it.

1. There is a state flag, mountain, tree, and bird.

2. Hawaii is 500 times bigger than Rhode Island.

3. More than half the states have people of Native American origin.

4. The state with the lowest population is Hawaii.

5. Each state has a flag with stripes that have a special meaning.

6. People often named states after where they came from.

DISCUSSION

Discuss the answers to the questions with your classmates.
1. Why did the states want to form a nation?
2. What are the flag, tree, bird, and flower of the state you are in?
3. What should be the fifty-first state? Why?

WRITING

Write four sentences about the United States or your country.

EXAMPLE:

My country is Bolivia. It is in South America. It has a population of about eight million. There are the Andes mountains, hills, and high flat land.

_____

_____

 DID YOU KNOW . . . ?
The official drink of Ohio is tomato juice. Florida's is orange juice.

The Buffalo

PREREADING

Answer the questions.

1. What is the name of the animal in the picture?
2. Where can you see this animal?
3. How big do you think this animal is?

The Buffalo

The buffalo is the largest North American animal. It can weigh more than 2,000 pounds. It lives in **a herd of** buffalo. Two hundred years ago, there were 60 million buffalo. They lived **all over** the **center** of North America. There were thousands of herds. One herd was 20 miles (32 kilometers) long and 20 miles wide. The buffalo **followed** the grass and the Native American Indians followed the buffalo.

The Native Americans used the buffalo for many things. They used it for meat. Sometimes they ate fresh meat. Sometimes they dried the meat in the sun and ate it later. The Indians also used the skin, or hide of the buffalo, to make **leather**. From the hide they made tents, clothes, shoes, hats, and rope. They did not **waste** anything.

But times changed. People from other lands came to America. These **immigrants** crossed the country in wagon trains. They killed the buffalo for food and hides. More and more people came, and everyone wanted leather. **Hunters** with guns killed the buffalo only for their hides. They wasted everything else. These hunters were very good at their job. By 1900, there were fewer than thirty buffalo left alive.

Today, there are about 30,000 buffalo in America, but herds are very small. You can see them in states like Wyoming. Sometimes you can buy buffalo meat at a restaurant. But you will never see a herd of buffalo as big as a city.

VOCABULARY

 MEANING

Complete the sentences with words from the box.

| a herd of | center | leather | immigrants |
| all over | followed | waste | hunters |

1. People who move to another country to live there are _____.

2. _____ are people who follow and kill animals.

3. _____ is made from the skin of an animal.

4. When you don't use something in a useful way, you _____ it.

5. _____ animals is a group of cows, buffalo, or elephants that live together.

6. *Came* and *went after* mean the same as _____ .

7. The _____ of something is the middle of it.

8. *Everywhere* is the same as _____ .

⭐ USE

Work with a partner to answer the questions. Use complete sentences.

1. What kinds of things do people *waste*?
2. What are some things that are made from *leather*?
3. What is something you see *all over* your city?
4. Why do *immigrants* leave their countries?
5. Who do children usually *follow*?
6. What kinds of buildings are in the *center* of your city?

COMPREHENSION

⭐ LOOKING FOR MAIN IDEAS

Write the questions to the answers.

1. Where _____?

   The buffalo lived all over the center of North America.

2. Why _____?

   They followed the buffalo because they used them for many things.

3. Who _____?

   Hunters killed the buffalo for their hides.

4. How many _____?

   There are about 30,000 buffalo in America today.

⭐ LOOKING FOR DETAILS

Circle *T* if the sentence is true. Circle *F* if the sentence is false.

1.	The buffalo can weigh more than 2,000 pounds.	T	F
2.	Two hundred years ago, there were 30,000 buffalo.	T	F
3.	The buffalo followed the Indians.	T	F
4.	In 1900, there were fewer than thirty buffalo.	T	F
5.	Hunters killed the buffalo for their hides.	T	F
6.	You cannot eat buffalo meat in a restaurant today.	T	F

DISCUSSION

Discuss the answers to the questions with your classmates.
1. What other animals do people use for food and clothing?
2. How were the buffalo important to the Indians?
3. Why is the story of the buffalo important today?

WRITING

Write four sentences about an animal or a kind of animal.

EXAMPLE:

Dogs help humans in so many ways. They are our friends. They also protect us and our homes. Some dogs are guides for blind people.

DID YOU KNOW . . . ?
Buffalo Bill was a famous buffalo hunter. In eighteen months he shot
4,000 buffalo!

Texas

PREREADING

Answer the questions.

1. What do you see in the picture?
2. What do you know about Texas?

Texas

A long time ago Texas was part of Mexico. The Mexican government did not want any Americans to move to Texas. An American man named Stephen Austin brought a lot of people to Texas. They built towns. The Mexican government was not happy. The Americans did not want to be part of Mexico, and a war began. Many years passed. Finally, Texas was free. It became a state in 1836.

Texans are **proud of** their history. Many people from Mexico live in Texas today. They are an important part of the state's history. A popular kind of food in Texas is called "Tex-Mex." It is **a mixture of** American and Mexican food. Texas is also famous for its cowboys. These cowboys **ride horses** and take care of the cattle. They wear big hats and Western **boots**. When people think of Texas, they often think of cowboys.

One way to **describe** Texas is "big." In fact, Texas is the second biggest state. Only Alaska is bigger. Texas has more cattle and sheep than any other state. It has the most farms or ranches in the United States. It has the biggest **ranch** in the country, too. Texas also **produces** the most fruit and vegetables. It gives the United States one-third of American oil! That's why Texans "think big."

VOCABULARY

 MEANING

Complete the sentences with words from the box.

Texans	a mixture of	boots	ranch
proud of	ride horses	describe	produces

1. People _____ for transportation or for fun.

2. A _____ is a big farm with cows and horses.

3. When you tell what something is like, you _____ it.

 UNIT 3

4. A person who grows or supplies something _____ it.

5. You get _____ something when you put different things together.

6. You are _____ something when it gives you pleasure or satisfaction.

7. Shoes that cover your ankles and sometimes your legs are called _____.

8. _____ are people who live in Texas.

⭐ USE

Work with a partner to answer the questions. Use complete sentences.

1. What is something that makes you feel *proud*?
2. When do you wear *boots*?
3. How do you *describe* your city?
4. What does your country *produce*?
5. Where do you see people *ride horses*?
6. What is *a mixture of* foods you like?

COMPREHENSION

⭐ LOOKING FOR MAIN IDEAS

Circle the letter of the best answer.

1. Texas was _____.
   a. a part of Mexico
   b. always part of the United States
   c. the capital of Mexico

2. Texans _____.
   a. have no history
   b. never ride horses
   c. are proud of their history

3. When Texans describe their state, they say it is _____.
   a. big
   b. not very big
   c. the size of a big ranch

LOOKING FOR DETAILS

Circle *T* if the sentence is true. Circle *F* if the sentence is false.

1.	Texans fought against the Mexicans.	T	F
2.	Texas became a state in 1836.	T	F
3.	There were cowboys in Texas.	T	F
4.	Americans wanted to be part of Mexico.	T	F
5.	Alaska is bigger than Texas.	T	F
6.	Texas produces all of the oil in the United States.	T	F

DISCUSSION

Discuss the answers to the questions with your classmates.

1. What do you know about cowboys?
2. What special work clothes can you name? Who wears them?
3. What would you do if an oil company found oil in your backyard?

WRITING

Write four sentences about a state or a part of a country you know.

EXAMPLE:

Jalisco is a state in Mexico. It is a beautiful state with mountains, lakes, and beaches. The capital of Jalisco is Guadalajara. Guadalajara is in the center of Jalisco.

_____

_____

_____

_____

DID YOU KNOW . . . ?
The state of Texas is bigger than England.

 12   UNIT 3

The Story of Colonel Sanders

PREREADING

Answer the questions.

1. Who is the man in the picture?
2. Why is he famous?

The Story of Colonel* Sanders

Everybody knows Colonel Sanders. He's the gentleman with the white suit on the Kentucky Fried Chicken (KFC) box.

Harlan Sanders came from a poor family and started work at an early age. He worked at many jobs. In his last job as a gas station operator, he prepared food for **customers**. Soon people came for the food and not the gas. So Sanders bought a restaurant across the street. The restaurant became popular for its chicken. The **governor** of Kentucky gave Sanders the **honorary title** "Colonel" for giving the state a special food.

Some years later, Sanders needed to sell his restaurant. It was in the way of a new **interstate highway**. He decided to sell the *idea* of his chicken. He traveled the country and cooked his chicken for restaurants. If they liked it, they promised to give him 5 cents for every chicken they sold. Soon there were many restaurants selling Sanders's chicken. By 1964, Sanders had more than 600 **franchises**. He had one of the largest **fast-food chains** in the world!

In 1964, Sanders sold KFC for $2 million. He continued to tell people about his chicken and visited KFC restaurants around the world. He traveled 250,000 miles (402,336 kilometers) a year until he died in 1980 at the age of 90.

Today, many people around the world still **recognize** Colonel Sanders. There are more than 11,000 KFC restaurants around the world in more than 84 countries. His picture is on the sign outside every one of them.

*colonel: a top officer in the army

VOCABULARY

MEANING

Complete the sentences with words from the box.

customers	honorary title	franchise	chains
governor	interstate highway	fast food	recognize

1. The _____ is the top person in a U.S. state.

2. People who buy things from a business are its _____.

3. Many businesses with the same name that are owned by one person or company are part of _____.

4. When you _____ a person, you notice that you have seen or heard of him before.

5. Food that is prepared, served, and eaten quickly is _____.

6. An _____ is given to someone to show respect.

7. Businesses that have a specific company's name and sell its products are _____.

8. An _____ crosses more than one state.

USE

Work with a partner to answer the questions. Use complete sentences.

1. What is your favorite *fast food*?

2. What are some fast-food restaurants that people in your country *recognize*?

3. What are some other U.S. business *chains*?

4. What other *honorary titles* do you know?

5. What other *franchises* can you name?

6. What is an example of an *interstate highway*? Where does it start and end?

COMPREHENSION

 LOOKING FOR MAIN IDEAS

Circle the letter of the best answer.

1. Colonel Sanders owned a _____ chain.
    a. customer
    b. restaurant
    c. highway
2. His restaurants served _____ food.
    a. honorary
    b. state
    c. fast
3. He grew his business by creating _____.
    a. franchises
    b. chicken
    c. 5 cents

 LOOKING FOR DETAILS

***One* word or number in each sentence is *not* correct. Cross it out and write the correct answer above it.**

1. Colonel Sanders's picture is on Kentucky Fried Chicken suits.

2. Harlan Sanders started school at an early age.

3. The senator of Kentucky gave him an honorary title.

4. He decided to sell the idea of his title.

5. Restaurants paid him 5 times for each chicken they sold.

6. With 600 chickens, he had one of the largest fast-food chains in the world.

DISCUSSION

Discuss the answers to the questions with your classmates.

1. What are the favorite fast foods in your country?
2. Which U.S. fast-food franchises are there in your country?
3. What is good and what is bad about fast food?

WRITING

Write four sentences about your favorite fast-food restaurant.

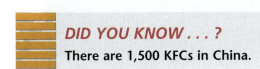

My favorite fast-food restaurant is Alligator Hut. They make great pizzas.

Their milk shakes are the best! Their meals are very cheap, too.

_____

_____

_____

_____

DID YOU KNOW . . . ?
There are 1,500 KFCs in China.

The President of the United States

PREREADING

Answer the questions.

1. Who is the president of the United States?
2. What other U.S. presidents do you know?
3. What are they famous for?

The President of the United States

Do you want to be president of the United States of America? Maybe you can apply for the job. Answer these three questions. Are you a U.S.-born **citizen**? Have you lived in the United States for at least fourteen years? Are you thirty-five years old or older? Did you say "yes" to all three questions? Then you can **take the first steps** to the White House.

You become president for a **term**. A term is four years. You can **serve** no more than two terms. This means that you can be president only twice. This became law in 1951. Before that, the law was different. **In fact**, Franklin D. Roosevelt became president in 1933. He was still president when he died in 1945. He was president for twelve years. No one was president longer than he was.

As president of the United States, you **earn** $400,000 a year. You also get an extra $50,000 for **expenses**, tax free. You have your own **limousine**, jet, and housekeepers—all free. You also live rent free, in the White House in Washington, D.C. You are head of the richest country in the world.

Past presidents of the United States included many different types of people. There were twenty-two lawyers, four soldiers, four farmers, four teachers, two writers, two businessmen, one engineer, one tailor, and one actor. Eight of them did not have a college education!

VOCABULARY

 **MEANING**

Complete the sentences with words from the box.

citizen	term	in fact	expenses
take (the first) steps	serve	earn	limousine

1. A specific period of time is a _____.

2. A _____ is an expensive car with a driver.

3. A person who was born in a country is a _____ of that country.

4. To _____ one's country or an organization is to work or do a useful job especially for it.

5. _____ is another way of saying *in truth*.

6. Your _____ are things you pay for like food, rent, or travel.

7. You _____ money when you work to get it.

8. To _____ is to start to take action to do something.

 **USE**

Work with a partner to answer the questions. Use complete sentences.

1. Of what country are you a *citizen*?

2. How much money would you like to *earn* one day?

3. What are your biggest *expenses*?

4. When do people use *limousines*?

5. In what jobs can a person *serve* another?

6. How many *terms* do you think a president should be able to serve? Why?

COMPREHENSION

⭐ LOOKING FOR MAIN IDEAS

Write complete answers to the questions.

1. What three things must you be to become president of the United States? _____

   _____

2. How long can you be president of the United States?

   _____

3. What kinds of people are presidents of the United States?

   _____

⭐ LOOKING FOR DETAILS

One **word in each sentence is** *not* **correct. Cross out the word and write the correct answer above it.**

1. To be president, you must be forty-five years old or older.

2. To be president, you must work in the United States for fourteen years.

3. A term is eight years.

4. Franklin D. Roosevelt was president for two terms.

5. Eight presidents did not have a high school education.

6. As president, you are the businessman of the richest country in the world.

DISCUSSION

Discuss the answers to the questions with your classmates.

1. What makes a good president?
2. Can a woman be president in your country?
3. What do you know about the current president of the United States?

WRITING

Write four sentences about a president or a famous leader.

EXAMPLE:

John F. Kennedy was president of the United States. He was the youngest president. He was also the first Catholic president. He died in 1963 when he was visiting Texas.

DID YOU KNOW . . . ?
No president was an only child.

Martin Luther King Jr.

PREREADING

Answer the questions.

1. Who is the man in the picture?
2. What is he famous for?

Martin Luther King Jr.

Martin Luther King Jr. was an African-American **clergyman** from Atlanta, Georgia. When King was a child, it was against the law for black people and white people to mix in **public places**. Black people sat in different parts of restaurants and movie theaters. Black people sat at the back of the bus. Black and white children went to different schools. This kind of separation is called *segregation*.

King loved to study. He was a good student and went to college when he was only fifteen years old. After he finished college, he began to fight segregation. He did not believe in **violence**. He believed in peace. He helped black people to **protest** in peace. They **went on marches** in peace.

King also wanted **equality** for everybody. He wanted black and white men and women to have an equal chance in the United States. This is called the *civil rights movement*. In 1963, King was the leader of the civil rights march on Washington, D.C. Thousands of people listened to his famous speech. It begins, "I have a dream."

In 1964, Martin Luther King Jr. was the youngest person to get the Nobel Peace Prize. This award is for people who try to **make peace** in the world. In 1968, an **assassin** killed King. He was only thirty-nine years old. His birthday, January 15th, is a national holiday in the United States.

VOCABULARY

 MEANING

Complete the sentences with words from the box.

clergyman	violence	went on marches	make peace
public places	protest	equality	assassin

1. A person who kills a politician or leader is an _____.

2. A Christian preacher is a _____.

3. _____ is when everybody has the same rights.

4. When people walked from one place to another to show they were not happy, they _____.

5. To _____ is to complain about a situation.

6. Places in towns or cities that are for all people are _____.

7. _____ is when someone uses force to hurt or harm. It is the opposite of peace.

8. When you _____, you want to be friends and not fight anymore.

⭐ USE

Work with a partner to answer the questions. Use complete sentences.

1. What are some *public places* in your town?
2. What shows on television have or show *violence*?
3. What do some people *protest* about?
4. Which countries should not fight with each other and *make peace*?
5. What kinds of *equality* are there today?
6. Who were some leaders killed by *assassins*?

COMPREHENSION

⭐ LOOKING FOR MAIN IDEAS

Circle the letter of the best answer.

1. In King's time, the South had _____.
   a. segregation
   b. white buses
   c. children's restaurants

2. *Civil rights* means _____.
   a. equality for everybody
   b. to be white
   c. equality for women only

3. January 15th is _____.
   a. the day King died
   b. the day King got the Nobel Peace Prize
   c. a national holiday

LOOKING FOR DETAILS

Circle *T* if the sentence is true. Circle *F* if the sentence is false.

1. King did not want to stop segregation.	T	F
2. Martin Luther King Jr. believed in peace.	T	F
3. In 1968, King got the Nobel Peace Prize.	T	F
4. King died when he was thirty-nine years old.	T	F
5. His famous speech begins, "I had a dream."	T	F
6. In 1963, he was the leader of a civil rights march.	T	F

DISCUSSION

Discuss the answers to the questions with your classmates.

1. What other famous people do you know who worked for peace?
2. People in the United States are free. What does this mean?
3. Who are some great leaders in your country? Why are they great?

WRITING

Write four sentences about a person who changed people's lives.

EXAMPLE:

Mother Teresa was a missionary. She lived in India and cared for the poor and sick. She got a Nobel Peace Prize. She died soon after her eighty-seventh birthday.

_____

_____

_____

_____

DID YOU KNOW...?
Martin Luther King Jr. was married and had three children.

Basketball

PREREADING

Answer the questions.

1. What are the people in the picture doing?
2. How do you play basketball?

Basketball

James Naismith invented basketball in 1891. Naismith was a Canadian, but he lived in the United States. He taught sports at Springfield Training School in the state of Massachusetts. He found there were no interesting **indoor** games to play in the winter months, so he thought of a game.

Naismith's students **played the game** of basketball for the first time in the Springfield **gym** in 1891. There were nine men on each **team**. They used a soccer ball. They put peach* baskets on the gym wall. The goal or purpose of the game was to throw the ball in the basket. That is why he called the game *basketball*. A man with a **ladder** went to the basket. He climbed the ladder and took the ball out of the basket. Luckily, only one man got the ball into the basket in the first game.

Basketball is a very fast game. Players run up and down the basketball **court** or gym floor the whole game. One team moves the ball to the basket. At the same time, players from the other team try to get the ball. When a player gets the ball in the basket, the team **scores** points. The team with the most points at the end wins the game.

Most players are tall. Many of them are over 7 feet tall and weigh more than 200 pounds. One of basketball's great players was Barney Sedran. He played from 1912 to 1926 and is in the Basketball Hall of Fame. He was only 5 feet 4 inches tall and 118 pounds!

Today, basketball is an **international sport**. In the United States, the National Basketball Association (NBA) has some of the best players in the world. Basketball is also an Olympic sport today. In the Olympics, the best teams from many countries play to show they are the best.

peach: a round, juicy orange fruit

VOCABULARY

MEANING

Complete the sentences with words from the box.

indoor	gym	ladder	scores
played the game	team	court	international sport

1. An _____ is played between two or more countries.

2. A team that _____ gets points toward winning the game.

3. The place where a game of basketball or tennis is played is a

   _____ .

4. People that _____ participated in a sport or game.

5. A game that happens inside a building is an _____ sport.

6. A _____ has steps to climb up or down.

7. _____ is short for gymnasium—a large hall for sports.

8. A group of people who play together is a _____ .

USE

Work with a partner to answer the questions. Use complete sentences.

1. What are some sports activities that people do in a *gym*?

2. What are the most popular *international* team *sports*?

3. What are some *indoor* winter games?

4. What sports do people play on a *court*?

5. What is the name of your favorite *team*?

6. What things do people do at a game when their team *scores*?

COMPREHENSION

 ## LOOKING FOR MAIN IDEAS

Circle the letter of the best answer.

1. James Naismith _____.
   a. invented a gym
   b. invented basketball
   c. liked peaches
2. The first game of basketball _____.
   a. used peach baskets
   b. was like soccer
   c. was in Canada
3. Today, basketball is _____.
   a. not an Olympic sport
   b. only played in the United States
   c. an international sport

 ## LOOKING FOR DETAILS

One word in each sentence is *not* correct. Cross out the word and write the correct answer above it.

1. There were ten men on each basketball team.

2. They used a gym ball.

3. Naismith was American.

4. They put peach balls on the gym wall.

5. Barney Sedran was one of basketball's first players.

6. Players climb up and down the court the whole game.

DISCUSSION

Discuss the answers to the questions with your classmates.

1. What sports can you name where you need a ball and you run?
2. In which sports is it good to be big? Why?
3. In which sports is it good to be small? Why?

WRITING

Write four sentences about a sport.

> **EXAMPLE:**
>
> The favorite sport in my country is soccer. My father and my brothers watch it on television all the time. My brothers and I also like to play soccer. We play soccer on the weekend.

DID YOU KNOW . . . ?

Naismith wrote the rules for the new game in about an hour. We still use most of them today.

Abraham Lincoln

PREREADING

Answer the questions.

1. Who is the man in the picture?
2. Why is he famous?

Abraham Lincoln

Abraham Lincoln was the sixteenth president of the United States. He was born in Kentucky in 1809. His family was very poor. When Lincoln was a boy, he worked on his family's farm. He did not go to school. He taught himself to read and write. Later, Lincoln studied law and became a **lawyer**. After that, he became a politician.

Everybody liked Abraham Lincoln because he was intelligent and **hardworking**. Lincoln was very **ambitious**. He wanted to be good at everything he did. He said that he wanted to win the "race of life." He was also kind and **honest**. People called him "Honest Abe."

Lincoln became president in 1860. In 1861, there was a war between the North and the South of the United States. The people in the South wanted a separate government from the United States. The North wanted the United States to stay together as one country. Lincoln was the **leader** of the North. In the war, brother killed brother. The Civil War was four years long.

The North won the **Civil War***. The war ended on April 9, 1865. Six days later, President Lincoln and his wife went to the theater. Inside the theater, a man went behind the president and **shot** him in the head. The man's name was John Wilkes Booth. He was a **supporter of** the South. Lincoln died the next morning.

Civil War: Civil War (capitalized) refers to the war in the U.S. from 1861 to 1865 between the northern and southern states, and *civil war* (lowercased) refers to any war in which opposing sides are from the same country.

VOCABULARY

MEANING

Complete the sentences with words from the box.

lawyer	ambitious	leader	shot
hardworking	honest	civil war	supporter of

1. You are _____ when you want to be the best at everything.
2. When you always tell the truth, you are _____.
3. You are a _____ when other people follow you.
4. A _____ an idea or an action believes in it.
5. A person who gives others advice about the law is a _____.
6. If a person _____ others, that person injured or killed them with a gun.
7. A war between two groups in a country is a _____. In the United States, the war between the North and the South was called the Civil War (with capital letters).
8. A person who works a lot is _____.

USE

Work with a partner to answer the questions. Use complete sentences.

1. What world organization are you a *supporter of*?
2. Who is a famous *leader* past or present?
3. Who is a *hardworking* person you know?
4. In which country was or is there a *civil war*?
5. Which person in the news do you think is not *honest*? Why?
6. Who is an *ambitious* person you know? How do you know this person is ambitious?

COMPREHENSION

 LOOKING FOR MAIN IDEAS

Write complete answers to the questions.

1. Why did everybody like Abraham Lincoln?

   _____

2. What facts about Lincoln show that he was hardworking?

   _____

3. Why did John Wilkes Booth shoot Lincoln?

   _____

 LOOKING FOR DETAILS

Circle *T* if the sentence is true. Circle *F* if the sentence is false.

1. Lincoln was born in 1860.	T	F
2. People called Lincoln "Honest Abe."	T	F
3. The Civil War started in 1860.	T	F
4. Lincoln was the leader of the North.	T	F
5. The Civil War ended in 1865.	T	F
6. Abraham Lincoln died in the war.	T	F

DISCUSSION

Discuss the answers to the questions with your classmates.

1. Abraham Lincoln's parents were poor. Do children of poor parents make better leaders? Why?
2. What qualities does a person need to be successful in school or at work?
3. What qualities make a good president?

WRITING

Write four sentences about an honest person.

EXAMPLE:

My brother is an honest person. Sometimes it is good. Sometimes it is bad.

It is good because I always know that what he says is the truth.

_____

_____

_____

_____

 DID YOU KNOW . . . ?
Abraham Lincoln was the tallest president. He was 6 feet 4 inches tall.

Washington, D.C.

PREREADING

Answer the questions.

1. What do you see in the pictures?
2. Where are these buildings?
3. What are some other famous buildings in this city?

Washington, D.C.

Washington, D.C., is the **capital of** the United States. It is an unusual city. It is a city that has no state. It is a **district**—the District of Columbia, or D.C. That is why it is called Washington, D.C.

George Washington became the first president of the United States in 1790. People wanted to have a capital city that was not a part of a state. Washington **picked** a place near his home, Mount Vernon, in the state of Virginia. The states of Maryland and Virginia gave some land to form Washington, D.C., named after George Washington.

The city of Washington, D.C., has **wide streets**, parks, and beautiful buildings. These buildings tell the history of the United States. One of the most famous buildings is the White House. This is the home of the president. Another important building is the **Capitol**. This is where Congress meets to make the laws of the country.

Washington, D.C., is very special in the spring. Japan sent more than 3,000 cherry trees* to the United States in 1912. The trees have beautiful flowers in March or April. It is a very pretty time to see Washington, D.C., because it is **cherry blossom time**.

Millions of people visit Washington, D.C. **Tourism** is an important **business**. The other main business is government. Every year the president sees the leaders of many countries in Washington, D.C.

cherry tree: a tree with very small, soft, red or yellow round fruit

VOCABULARY

 MEANING

Complete the sentences with words from the box.

capital of	picked	Capitol	tourism
district	wide streets	cherry blossom time	business

1. _____ are streets that are a long way from one side to the other.

2. The time when the cherry trees have flowers is _____ .

3. The _____ a country is the center of its government.

4. A _____ is a company that buys and sells things.

5. The _____ is the building where the U.S. Congress meets.

6. George Washington _____ a place near his home. This means he chose it.

7. A _____ is one part of a city or a country.

8. _____ is the business of providing services for tourists.

⭐ USE

Work with a partner to answer the questions. Use complete sentences.

1. What are *capitals of* some countries you know?
2. What is the name of a *wide street* in your town?
3. What American *business* do you find unusual?
4. What is the most expensive *district* in your city?
5. In what cities is there a lot of *tourism*?
6. How does Washington, D.C., look in *cherry blossom time*?

COMPREHENSION

⭐ LOOKING FOR MAIN IDEAS

Circle the letter of the best answer.

1. Washington, D.C., has no _____.
   a. city
   b. state
   c. district

2. George Washington _____.
   a. picked the place for the capital
   b. gave some land to Virginia
   c. did not want a capital city

3. The city of Washington, D.C., has _____.
   a. the homes of all the presidents
   b. no parks
   c. many famous places to see and things to do

LOOKING FOR DETAILS

Circle *T* if the sentence is true. Circle *F* if the sentence is false.

1.	Mount Vernon was George Washington's home.	T	F
2.	Virginia was not a state.	T	F
3.	The Capitol is another name for the White House.	T	F
4.	Congress meets in the White House.	T	F
5.	Cherry trees are beautiful but have no flowers.	T	F
6.	Tourism is the only business in Washington, D.C.	T	F

DISCUSSION

Discuss the answers to the questions with your classmates.

1. How do you describe a capital city you visited?
2. What important buildings do you find in a capital city?
3. What are some reasons why people pick a particular city to be the capital?

WRITING

Write four sentences about the capital city of your country.

EXAMPLE:

Tokyo is the capital of my country. It is the largest city in Japan. Tokyo has a population of about 13 million. Tokyo Tower is a popular site for tourists.

_____

_____

_____

DID YOU KNOW . . . ?

More than 100 nations have embassies in Washington, D.C.

Halloween

PREREADING

Answer the questions.

1. What things do you see in the picture? Describe them.
2. What do you know about Halloween?

Halloween

On October 31st, Americans celebrate Halloween. Halloween means "holy" (*hallow*) "evening" (*een*). This is the evening before the Christian holy day of All **Saints** Day. On All Saints Day, Christians remember the saints. But Halloween is older than Christianity.

Before Christianity, people in Europe believed that on October 31st **ghosts** of dead people came back. To **scare** the ghosts, people dressed like **devils** and were very noisy. They also made big fires to scare the ghosts away. Later, people did not believe in ghosts, but they celebrated the day of Halloween for fun.

Immigrants came from Europe to America and brought with them the custom of Halloween. Halloween has some strange symbols. One symbol is a jack-o'-lantern. The jack-o'-lantern is to scare the ghosts. People cut a hole in the top of a pumpkin,* throw away all of the inside, and cut a face in the pumpkin. Then they put a candle inside to make the face light up.

Today, in the United States, Halloween is very popular with children. They wear **masks** and special costumes. They want to look like **skeletons** and ghosts. Then they go from house to house and say, "Trick or **treat**!" People give them candies, cookies, or fruit. When people give nothing, the children sometimes **play tricks** on them.

*pumpkin: a large, round, orange vegetable

VOCABULARY

 MEANING

Complete the sentences with words from the box.

saints	scare	masks	treat
ghosts	devils	skeletons	play tricks

1. People without bodies who come back after they die are _____.

2. To frighten is to _____.

3. _____ are covers for the face.

4. _____ are the bones that make our bodies.

5. _____ are men or women who receive a special honor by the Christian church after they die because they lived holy lives.

6. We say that very bad people or spirits are _____.

7. When you do things to make someone look stupid, you _____ on that person.

8. A _____ is something special that makes you happy.

⭐ USE

Work with a partner to answer the questions. Use complete sentences.

1. What is your favorite *treat*?
2. What *scares* you?
3. Do you know people who *play tricks*? What tricks do they play?
4. When do people wear *masks*?
5. Where do you see pictures or statues of *saints*?
6. Do you think some places have *ghosts*? Why?

COMPREHENSION

⭐ LOOKING FOR MAIN IDEAS

Circle the letter of the best answer.

1. On October 31st, Americans celebrate _____.
   a. All Saints Day
   b. Halloween
   c. Christianity

2. _____ from Europe brought Halloween to the United States.
   a. Saints
   b. Immigrants
   c. Children

3. Today, Halloween is _____.
   a. popular with children
   b. for people who give nothing
   c. for special people

Circle *T* if the sentence is true. Circle *F* if the sentence is false.

1. All Saints Day is the day before Halloween.   T   F
2. Halloween began after Christianity.   T   F
3. Halloween came from Europe.   T   F
4. A jack-o'-lantern is a pumpkin with a face.   T   F
5. On Halloween, children want to look like skeletons.   T   F
6. On Halloween, people play tricks on children.   T   F

DISCUSSION

Discuss the answers to the questions with your classmates.

1. Is there a day like Halloween in your country? How is it the same? How is it different?
2. What are some U.S. holidays or special days you know? How do people celebrate them?
3. Do you believe in ghosts? Why?

WRITING

Write four sentences about a custom you know about.

> **EXAMPLE:**
>
> *The Day of the Dead is a special day in Mexico. It is in November. We remember our dead relatives and friends on this day. We make special food for the dead.*

_____

_____

_____

_____

DID YOU KNOW . . . ?
Ninety-nine percent of the pumpkins sold in the United States become jack-o'-lanterns.

Native Americans

PREREADING

Answer the questions.

1. What do you know about Native Americans in the United States?
2. Why do many people call them Indians?

Native Americans

There were about 1 million Native American people in North America when Christopher Columbus arrived in 1492. Columbus thought he was in India. He called the people with **dark skin** *Indians*. This was a mistake, but the name *Indian* stuck.

There were more than 2,000 different groups of Native American people at the time of Columbus. Each **tribe** had a different name. Each tribe also had a different language and **customs**. But all these people could speak with each other in one language—**sign language**. All these people also thought in the same way. They believed that the land and waters **belonged to** everybody.

The people who came from Europe after Columbus did not understand the first, or native, Americans. Many of them thought the Indians were **savages**. They were afraid of them. For the next 400 years they fought with each other. They fought about who owned the land and how to use it.

The tribes **lost** their land, and the U.S. government made them live on **reservations**. Reservations were tax-free areas of land "reserved for" the Native Americans. The government gave them food because they could not hunt and find food for themselves. There was no work for them. In 1924 a law made Native Americans citizens of the United States. Today some Indian tribes choose to live by their old customs, and some do not.

VOCABULARY

 MEANING

Complete the sentences with words from the box.

dark skin	customs	belonged to	lost
tribe	sign language	savages	reservations

1. People who use their hands to speak use _____.

2. Wild or uncivilized people are _____.

3. A _____ is a group of people led by a chief.

4. Areas of land for Native Americans to live on are _____.

5. Things that were yours or were your property _____ you.

6. Skin that looks brown or black is _____.

7. Certain ways of doing things that are special to a group of people or a nation are _____.

8. If someone _____ something, he or she does not have it anymore.

 USE

Work with a partner to answer the questions. Use complete sentences.

1. In which countries do most people have *dark skin*?
2. Who uses *sign language*?
3. What are two things that *belong to* you?
4. What is an old *custom* you like and still do today?
5. What are some other *tribes* of people that you know about?
6. What is something you *lost*? What happened?

COMPREHENSION

 LOOKING FOR MAIN IDEAS

Circle the letter of the best answer.

1. Columbus thought he was in _____.
   a. North America
   b. the United States
   c. India

2. All Native Americans _____.
   a. thought in the same way
   b. had the same customs for all tribes
   c. were one tribe

3. Many Native Americans _____.
   a. are not U.S. citizens
   b. live on reservations
   c. give food to the government

★ LOOKING FOR DETAILS

Circle *T* if the sentence is true. Circle *F* if the sentence is false.

1. Columbus went to India.	T	F
2. There were more than 1 million tribes in North America at the time of Columbus.	T	F
3. Each tribe had a different language.	T	F
4. The tribes used sign language to speak with each other.	T	F
5. The new Americans and the Indians fought for 400 years.	T	F
6. Native Americans became U.S. citizens in 1924.	T	F

DISCUSSION

Discuss the answers to the questions with your classmates.

1. What did you learn from this unit about Native Americans?
2. In what other countries are there tribes of people?
3. What is the most interesting tribe you know? Why is it the most interesting?

WRITING

Write four sentences about a tribe or a group of people.

> **EXAMPLE:**
>
> *The Inuit live in the coldest areas of the world. They were called Inuit*
>
> *Eskimos, but they wanted to change their name to Inuit. This means*
>
> *"human beings." The Inuit have special customs.*

_____

_____

_____

_____

DID YOU KNOW . . . ?

The Native Americans didn't have horses at the time of Columbus. The Spanish settlers brought horses (and guns!) with them from Europe. Horses changed the lives of the Native Americans.

A First Look at New England

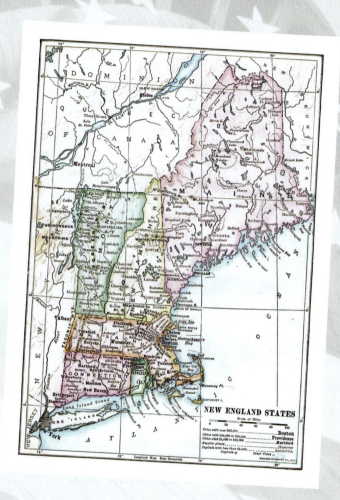

NEW ENGLAND STATES

PREREADING

Answer the questions.

1. Are the New England states on the east or west side of the United States?

2. How many New England states are there?

A First Look at New England

People often talk about parts of the United States as the "South," the "West," the "Mid-West," or "New England." What is New England? New England is a region of six states: Maine, New Hampshire, Massachusetts, Rhode Island, Connecticut, and Vermont.

New England is not very big. It is about one third the size of Texas, but New England is important in history. New England is the oldest part of the United States. Some of the first English **colonies** started there, and the American **Revolution** began in New England.

How did New England get its name? An **Englishman** named John Smith came to America in 1614. He **explored** the coast of Maine and Massachusetts. He thought about England when he saw the land. He made a **map** of the area and named it *New England*. The **Pilgrims** followed his map when they came to the United States. Soon everybody used the name *New England* for this part of America.

Later, when the United States was born, New England became the center of **culture**. Important art, **literature**, and science came from this area. The first important schools started there. Harvard University started in Cambridge, Massachusetts, in 1636. Later, people from New England went to live in other parts of the country. They took New England ideas and culture with them.

VOCABULARY

 **MEANING**

Complete the sentences with words from the box.

colonies	Englishman	map	culture
revolution	explored	pilgrims	literature

1. John Smith traveled around the coast of Massachusetts and Maine to see what it was like. This means he _____ it.

2. New places where people move that have the laws and leaders of their old country are called _____.

3. A _____ is the beliefs, ideas, values, and knowledge a group of people share from history.

4. The first U.S. settlers from Europe were _____. They came to the United States because of their beliefs about religion and God.

5. A _____ happens when people are unhappy and fight their leaders.

6. The books and other written things in a culture are its _____.

7. A picture or drawing of a place that shows you where other places and things are is a _____.

8. A man from England is called an _____.

⭐ USE

Work with a partner to answer the questions. Use complete sentences.

1. What is the difference between a *map* and a picture?
2. What other countries do you know that were *colonies*? What countries did they belong to?
3. What famous *literature* from your country do you like to read?
4. What other parts of the world do you want to *explore*?
5. In what other countries are there *pilgrims*? Where do they go?
6. Describe the *culture* of your country.

COMPREHENSION

⭐ LOOKING FOR MAIN IDEAS

Circle the letter of the best answer.

1. New England is the _____ part of the United States.
   a. one third
   b. English
   c. oldest

2. New England is an important place in _____.
   a. U.S. history
   b. Massachusetts
   c. the western United States

3. New England became the _____ of culture of the United States.

   a. states

   b. section

   c. center

 LOOKING FOR DETAILS

One word in each sentence is *not* correct. Cross out the word and write the correct answer above it.

1. New England is six parts.

2. New England is about one half the size of Texas.

3. New England is important in revolution.

4. The first English colonies explored there.

5. John Smith was an English.

6. He made a picture of the area.

DISCUSSION

Discuss the answers to the questions with your classmates.

1. Why were the first English colonies started on the east coast of the United States?

2. What do you know about the American Revolution?

3. Where are the centers of culture in the United States today?

WRITING

Write four sentences about the town, city, or state where you live.

EXAMPLE:

I live in San Francisco. It is in the state of California. It is on the west

coast of the United States. Many immigrants come to San Francisco

because it has a good climate.

_____

_____

_____

_____

DID YOU KNOW . . . ?

Connecticut is also a Native American name meaning "place of the long river."
This refers to the Connecticut River that goes from northern to southern
Connecticut.

Thomas Jefferson

PREREADING

Answer the questions.

1. Who do you see in the picture?
2. What was his job?

Thomas Jefferson

Thomas Jefferson was a man of many **talents**. He was a musician, an inventor, an **architect**, a lawyer, a politician, and one of the first archaeologists.* He also read and collected many books. His **library** had 6,000 books and later became the Library of Congress.** He even designed his own house, Monticello. However, Jefferson is best known as the main **author** of the **Declaration** of Independence, one of the most important documents in the history of the United States. The leaders of the colonies signed the Declaration on July 4, 1776.

In 1800, Jefferson became the third president of the United States. He served for two terms. During his time as president, he bought a huge piece of land from the French. This **doubled** the size of the United States. He also organized an **expedition** to explore America's west.

In 1809, Jefferson **retired** to his home in Monticello. He spent his time working for the University of Virginia. He raised money to start the university, he designed the buildings and furniture for it, and he chose the teachers and the subjects.

Thomas Jefferson died on July 4, 1826. He died fifty years after he signed the Declaration of Independence. John Adams, the second president and another important author of the Declaration, died almost at the same minute on the same day.

* *archaeologists*: scientists who study people and countries from very long ago by looking at their tools, buildings, and graves
**Library of Congress*: the library of the United States

VOCABULARY

 MEANING

Complete the sentences with words from the box.

| talents | library | declaration | expedition |
| architect | author | doubled | retired |

1. If something became two times bigger than it was, it _____.
2. A _____ is a room or building for books.
3. A person who writes a book or a document is an _____.
4. Someone who can do some things without having to learn them first has _____.
5. A person who worked for many years and then stopped is _____.
6. An _____ is a long and carefully organized trip.
7. A _____ is something very important you say or write.
8. A person who makes the drawings for a building is an _____.

 USE

Work with a partner to answer the questions. Use complete sentences.

1. What *talents* do you have?
2. What will you do when you are *retired*?
3. Who is your favorite *author*?
4. What is a famous *library* in your country?
5. Who is a famous *architect* in your country? What kinds of buildings does she or he design?
6. What is a famous *expedition* you know about?

COMPREHENSION

 LOOKING FOR MAIN IDEAS

Circle the letter of the correct answer.

1. Thomas Jefferson was the main _____ of the Declaration
   of Independence.
   a. archaeologist
   b. politician
   c. author

2. He was a man of many _____ .
   a. inventors
   b. talents
   c. expeditions

3. He was a very _____ person.
   a. tired
   b. ambitious
   c. lazy

 LOOKING FOR DETAILS

Circle *T* if the sentence is true. Circle *F* if the sentence is false.

1. Thomas Jefferson lived in the Library of Congress.	T	F
2. His library became the Library of Congress.	T	F
3. The Declaration of Independence was signed on July 4, 1776.	T	F
4. Thomas Jefferson served two years as president of the United States.	T	F
5. He retired to the University of Vermont.	T	F
6. Thomas Jefferson and John Adams died on the same day.	T	F

DISCUSSION

Discuss the answers to the questions with your classmates.

1. What do you know about the Declaration of Independence?
2. Who was the first president of the United States?
3. What other famous government buildings in the United States can you name?

WRITING

Write four sentences about an important person in politics.

EXAMPLE:

Winston Churchill was a man of many talents. He was a soldier, a newspaper reporter, an author, an artist, and prime minister of England. He was a great leader of his people in time of war. People remember him for his courage and important things he said during the war.

_____

_____

_____

_____

_____

DID YOU KNOW . . . ?

Thomas Jefferson was the first president to shake hands instead of bowing to people.

Beverly Hills

PREREADING

Answer the questions.

1. What do you see in the picture?
2. Why is Beverly Hills famous?

Beverly Hills

Most visitors to Los Angeles, California, want to see Beverly Hills. This is where the homes of many movie stars are, but Beverly Hills is not Los Angeles. It is a small city next to Los Angeles.

All kinds of **celebrities** live in Beverly Hills. These celebrities are movie stars, television stars, **sports stars**, and other people in the news. Tourists can buy special maps of the homes of the stars. These homes are very beautiful. They usually have swimming pools and **tennis courts**. The homes have high walls or trees around them so sometimes you cannot see very much.

Beverly Hills is also famous for Rodeo Drive. This is one of the most expensive **shopping streets** in the United States. Rodeo Drive became an **elegant** street in the 1960s. Many famous stores opened on the street. People liked all the new styles and fashions that were there. Today, you can find the most expensive and unusual clothing, **jewelry**, and furniture in the world on Rodeo Drive. When you want to park your car in **public parking** on Rodeo Drive, an **attendant** will come and park your car for you.

Beverly Hills is really a small city. Only about 35,000 people live there. But during the day more than 200,000 people come to Beverly Hills to work or to shop!

VOCABULARY

 MEANING

Complete the sentences with words from the box.

celebrities	tennis courts	elegant	public parking
sports stars	shopping streets	jewelry	attendant

1. A place where people can park their cars is _____.

2. _____ are famous people.

3. A person who works in a parking lot and parks your car for you is an _____.

4. _____ is decorations usually made of gold, silver, or diamonds that people wear on their clothes or bodies.

5. Famous people in sports are _____.

6. Something beautiful, stylish, and usually expensive is _____.

7. Marked areas where people play tennis are _____.

8. Streets with a lot of shops are _____.

★ USE

Work with a partner to answer the questions. Use complete sentences.

1. What *jewelry* do you like to wear?
2. Where do you see a *tennis court*?
3. Who are some *celebrities* you know about?
4. Where is there *public parking* in your city?
5. Who are some famous *sports stars*?
6. What is the name of a *shopping street* in your town?

COMPREHENSION

★ LOOKING FOR MAIN IDEAS

Circle the letter of the best answer.

1. In Beverly Hills you can find _____.
   a. Los Angeles
   b. the homes of the movie stars
   c. the homes of tourists
2. The homes of celebrities have _____.
   a. no trees and tennis courts
   b. maps on them
   c. swimming pools and tennis courts
3. Rodeo Drive _____.
   a. is an expensive shopping street
   b. has no parking
   c. has only clothing stores

One word or number in each sentence is *not* correct. Cross it out and write the correct answer above it.

1. The houses have tennis stores.

2. Beverly Hills is a sports city.

3. The homes of the stars have small walls.

4. On Rodeo Drive, a celebrity will come and park your car for you.

5. About 200,000 people live in Beverly Hills.

6. Tourists can buy jewelry of the homes of the stars.

DISCUSSION

Discuss the answers to the questions with your classmates.

1. Imagine you are a famous person. What does your home look like?
2. Why do so many rich people want to live in the same town?
3. Imagine that you win $1 million. You have one hour to spend it on Rodeo Drive. What will you buy?

WRITING

Write four sentences about a popular city in your country.

> **EXAMPLE:**
>
> _Puerto Vallarta is a popular city in my country, Mexico. It is not a big city._
>
> _Many tourists go there because it is by the ocean and it is sunny all year._
>
> _They stay in the big hotels with beaches._

DID YOU KNOW . . . ?

Some people say _Bijan_ on Rodeo Drive is the most expensive store for men's clothing in the world. Customers need to make an appointment to get in. The average customer spends $100,000!

Theodore Roosevelt

PREREADING

Answer the questions.

1. Who is the man in the picture?
2. Why is he famous?

Theodore Roosevelt

Theodore Roosevelt was the twenty-sixth president of the United States. He was president from 1901 to 1909. He was a very **intelligent** man. He was also very **energetic**. He was a boxer, a soldier, a **rancher**, and an **explorer**.

This powerful man was not strong when he was a boy. He had problems with his breathing. He had **asthma**. His father wanted him to be strong. Roosevelt learned to box, and he played many other sports. Soon Roosevelt became strong and energetic.

After he became president, Roosevelt kept his body strong. He even boxed in the White House. One day, another boxer hit him in the eye. After that accident, Roosevelt became **blind** in one eye.

Theodore Roosevelt's **nickname** was "Teddy." Everybody called him Teddy. When he was president, he often liked **to hunt**. One day he went hunting with some friends and saw a small bear. He did not shoot the bear. He said the bear was too small and needed to go free. The next day the story of the little bear was in the newspapers. The newspapers named the little bear "Teddy" after the president. Soon people called toy bears for children "teddy bears."

When he left the White House, Teddy Roosevelt went to hunt in Africa. He then went to South America to explore places that nobody knew about. Everybody loved his energy.

VOCABULARY

 **MEANING**

Complete the sentences with words from the box.

intelligent	rancher	asthma	nickname
energetic	explorer	blind	to hunt

1. A person who owns and works on a very large farm is a

   _____ .

2. A silly name or a shorter form of someone's real name is a

   _____ .

3. _____ is a medical condition that makes breathing difficult

   at times.

4. An _____ person is full of life and is very active.

5. An _____ likes to travel to places to discover something.

6. Someone who likes to chase and catch or kill animals for sport likes

   _____ .

7. A person who knows and understands many things is _____ .

8. _____ means unable to see.

 USE

Work with a partner to answer the questions. Use complete sentences.

1. What are some of your friends' *nicknames*?
2. What kinds of people are *energetic*?
3. Is it right *to hunt* animals for sport?
4. What are some characteristics of an *intelligent* person?
5. What famous *explorers* can you name?
6. What does a *rancher* do?

COMPREHENSION

LOOKING FOR MAIN IDEAS

Circle the letter of the best answer.

1. Theodore Roosevelt was _____.
   a. not intelligent
   b. very energetic
   c. president for twenty-six years
2. Theodore Roosevelt's nickname was _____.
   a. Teddy
   b. Teddy Bear
   c. Little Bear
3. When he was a boy, Roosevelt _____.
   a. wanted to be president
   b. was not strong
   c. had a problem with his father

LOOKING FOR DETAILS

Circle *T* if the sentence is true. Circle *F* if the sentence is false.

1. Theodore Roosevelt was a rancher.	T	F
2. When he was young, Theodore had asthma.	T	F
3. Roosevelt hit a president in the eye.	T	F
4. Roosevelt had bears in the White House.	T	F
5. People called toy bears "teddy bears."	T	F
6. Teddy Roosevelt went to hunt in South America.	T	F

DISCUSSION

Discuss the answers to the questions with your classmates.

1. Why do sick people often do great things?
2. What is good and what is bad about hunting?
3. What are good nicknames for the other students in your class?

WRITING

Write four sentences about an energetic person you know.

EXAMPLE:

My mother is an energetic person. She takes care of all the family and

manages our home. She also works a full-time job. We help with things

around the house, but her energy keeps us going.

_____

_____

_____

_____

DID YOU KNOW . . . ?

Theodore Roosevelt was the first president to travel outside the United States during his term.

Niagara Falls

PREREADING

Answer the questions.

1. What do you see in the picture? Describe it.
2. Where is it located?

Niagara Falls

Niagara Falls is on **the border of** the United States and Canada. The falls are not the highest or oldest, but they are the most powerful in the United States. In 1803, Jerome Bonaparte, nephew of Napoleon, visited the falls with his new bride. After that Niagara Falls became the place to go for a honeymoon.* Today about 50,000 newlyweds go there every year, along with millions of other tourists.

During warm months, tourists can go on a boat to see the falls from the river. The boat comes very close to the bottom of the falls. People can feel the **mist** from the falling water. Tourists can also walk through a **tunnel** under the falls and look at the falls from behind.

Niagara Falls has **fascinated** people for a long time. Many have tried to cross the falls or go down them in different ways. In 1859, a Frenchman known as "The Great Blondin" was the first person to go across Niagara Falls on a **tightrope**. Later he did it **blindfolded**. Then he did it on stilts.** Finally, he went halfway across and stopped to have breakfast. He cooked some eggs, ate them, and then crossed to the other side. However, not everyone was successful. Today, **stunts** are illegal on the falls.

Niagara Falls is not just for honeymooners and stuntmen. It is one of the most **spectacular** and beautiful places in the world.

* *honeymoon*: vacation of a newly married couple
** *stilts*: a long pair of poles with places for the feet so that people can walk high above the ground

VOCABULARY

⭐ MEANING

Complete the sentences with words from the box.

| the border of | tunnel | tightrope | stunts |
| mist | fascinated | blindfolded | spectacular |

1. A _____ is a walkway or road that goes through something such as a mountain.

2. _____ two countries is the place where they meet.

3. With a cloth tied over your eyes so you cannot see, you are _____ .

4. Something that is very exciting to see or watch is _____ .

5. Dangerous actions done to entertain people are _____ .

6. If people have stopped and looked at something because it is so beautiful or interesting, it has _____ them.

7. A rope between two high points is called a _____ .

8. Air that is filled with small drops of water is called _____ .

⭐ USE

Work with a partner to answer the questions. Use complete sentences.

1. What *stunts* have you seen?
2. When are people sometimes *blindfolded*?
3. What unusual things have *fascinated* you?
4. Have you ever been in a *tunnel*? Describe your experience.
5. Where else might you see a *tightrope*?
6. What do you usually find at *the border of* a country?

COMPREHENSION

 LOOKING FOR MAIN IDEAS

Circle the letter of the best answer.

1. Niagara Falls is on the border of the United States and _____ .
   a. Greenland
   b. Mexico
   c. Canada
2. People often go there on a _____ .
   a. stilts
   b. stuntmen
   c. honeymoon
3. The Great Blondin cooked and ate his _____ halfway across the falls.
   a. blindfold
   b. tightrope
   c. breakfast

 LOOKING FOR DETAILS

Circle *T* if the sentence is true. Circle *F* if the sentence is false.

1. The Niagara Falls are the highest and the oldest falls in the United States.	T	F
2. The Niagara Falls are the most powerful in the United States.	T	F
3. Napoleon visited the falls.	T	F
4. You can take a boat ride over the falls.	T	F
5. You can walk through a tunnel under and behind the falls.	T	F
6. Stunts on the falls are illegal today.	T	F

DISCUSSION

Discuss the answers to the questions with your classmates.

1. What other falls can you name in the United States or another country?
2. What stunt would you like to do over the falls?
3. What meal would you cook and eat halfway across?

WRITING

Write four sentences about a spectacular stunt you have seen.

> **EXAMPLE:**
>
> *First, The Great Bonzo studied everything. He measured distances and weighed his equipment and himself. Next, he rode his bicycle to the starting point. Finally, he pedaled as fast as he could and jumped his mountain bike over my car.*

DID YOU KNOW . . . ?

The first person to go over Niagara Falls in a barrel and survive was a sixty-three-year-old female schoolteacher in 1901.

Harriet Tubman

PREREADING

Answer the questions.

1. Why do we say African American?
2. What is a slave?

Harriet Tubman

Harriet Tubman was born around 1820 in the South of the United States. She was an African American and a **slave**. In those days in the South, African Americans were slaves. People bought slaves to work in their houses, farms, and fields. Their **masters** bought and sold them like **property**. When Harriet became a young woman, she wanted to be free. She wanted **to escape** to the North of the United States. Everyone in the North was free.

Harriet Tubman escaped from the South to the North on the **Underground** Railroad. The Underground Railroad was not a real railroad. It was a **secret** organization of people. These people helped slaves to escape. At night, they took the slaves to a **safe** house. The slaves hid there. The next night, they took the slaves to the next house or "station" on the railroad. The word *underground* can mean "secret". This is why people called the organization the Underground Railroad.

When Harriet Tubman was free, she decided to help slaves. She joined the Underground Railroad, and soon she became its leader. It was a very dangerous job. She went back to the South time after time. She brought back slaves to freedom in the North. Before Harriet Tubman died in 1913, she helped 300 slaves to escape. She helped these people begin new lives as free men and women. Today, we honor the name of this **brave** woman.

VOCABULARY

 **MEANING**

Complete the sentences with words from the box.

slave	property	underground	safe
masters	to escape	secret	brave

1. Something that only certain people know about is a _____.
2. _____ is to get away from a place you do not want to be.
3. If you are in a place where no one can hurt you, you are in a _____ place.
4. A _____ is a person who belongs to someone else and works for no money.
5. A secret group that only a few people know about is an _____ organization.
6. People who own other people are called _____.
7. A _____ person is not afraid of anything.
8. Things that you own are your _____.

 **USE**

Work with a partner to answer the questions. Use complete sentences.

1. Who are some *brave* people you know?
2. What other words like *master* do you know?
3. Why do people have *secrets*?
4. Why were houses called *safe*?
5. Why was it wrong to own people as *property*?
6. What stories do you know about people who wanted *to escape*?

COMPREHENSION

 ## LOOKING FOR MAIN IDEAS

Circle the letter of the best answer.

1. Harriet Tubman wanted to be _____.
   a. a slave
   b. free
   c. an African American
2. The Underground Railroad was _____.
   a. a secret organization
   b. a real railroad
   c. a house in the North
3. Harriet Tubman _____.
   a. was dangerous
   b. had slaves
   c. helped slaves

 ## LOOKING FOR DETAILS

Circle *T* if the sentence is true. Circle *F* if the sentence is false.

1. Harriet was born in the North of the United States.	T	F
2. African Americans in the South were slaves.	T	F
3. Harriet wanted to escape to the South.	T	F
4. *Underground* also means "secret."	T	F
5. Harriet became the leader of the Underground Railroad.	T	F
6. Harriet helped 130 slaves to escape.	T	F

DISCUSSION

Discuss the answers to the questions with your classmates.

1. Why is it good to be free?
2. What kind of work did slaves do?
3. What brave people can you name? What did they do?

WRITING

Write four sentences about a secret.

> **EXAMPLE:**
>
> _It was my birthday, and I was seven. I wanted a bicycle, but my parents were_
> _poor. I did not know that my mom had saved the money to buy me one. That_
> _was her secret, and it made me very happy._

_____

_____

_____

_____

DID YOU KNOW . . . ?

In 1896, Harriet Tubman bought land next to her home and started a home for old people. She died there at the age of ninety-two or ninety-three.

The Boston Tea Party

THE DESTRUCTION OF TEA AT BOSTON HARBOR.

PREREADING

Answer the questions.

1. What are the people in the picture doing?
2. Why do you think they are doing it?

The Boston Tea Party

The American **colonists** were angry. The British government made them **pay taxes**. The colonists paid the taxes, but there was no one in the British government to speak for them. They **complained** and questioned the laws. The British wanted the colonists **to obey** them and not ask questions. Then, in 1773, the British passed the Tea **Act**. It said that the colonists could only buy their tea from the East India Company of England. The colonists were very angry. They wanted to buy tea from other companies.

On December 16, 1773, some colonists decided to do something to show their anger. Late that night, a group of fifty men **dressed up** as Native Americans. They went **on board** three East India tea ships. They threw all of the tea into the water. This was called "The Boston Tea Party."

The British King was very angry. He said, "Close Boston Harbor!" No food or other necessary things could enter Boston. The king also sent 4,000 soldiers to Boston—one British soldier for every four Bostonians! The king thought he could make the Bostonians obey the law, but he was wrong. The other colonies **felt sorry for** the Bostonians. They sent food and money. Slowly, the thirteen separate colonies began to unite against the British, and the American Revolution began. In 1776, Thomas Jefferson wrote the Declaration of Independence.

VOCABULARY

 MEANING

Complete the sentences with words from the box.

colonists	complained	act	on board
pay taxes	to obey	dressed up	felt sorry for

1. If you walk onto a ship or plane, you go _____.
2. If you wore nice clothes that are different from what you normally wear you _____.

3. If people said they were unhappy or annoyed, they _____ .

4. An _____ is a kind of law.

5. People who live in another person's land, where the laws and government are from their country back home, are _____ .

6. When people give a part of their money to the government, they _____ .

7. When someone was in trouble and you felt sad about it, you _____ him.

8. To do what someone else says is _____ .

⭐ USE

Work with a partner to answer the questions. Use complete sentences.

1. Why do people become *colonists*?

2. Why is it not good to *complain*?

3. Why is it not a good idea *to obey* without thinking?

4. Who are some people you *feel sorry for*?

5. What are some things you do when you go *on board* a ship or an airplane?

6. When do you *dress up*?

COMPREHENSION

⭐ LOOKING FOR MAIN IDEAS

Circle the letter of the best answer.

1. The Boston Tea Party was _____ .
   a. to celebrate the king's birthday
   b. paid for by the East India Company
   c. the start of the American Revolution

2. The colonists were angry because the British made them _____ .
   a. drink tea
   b. pay taxes
   c. close Boston Harbor

3. They were also angry because they had no one to _____ .
   a. drink more tea
   b. dress up as Native Americans
   c. speak for them in the British Government

 LOOKING FOR DETAILS

One word in each sentence is _not_ correct. Cross out the word and write the correct answer above it.

1. The British governor forced the colonists to pay taxes.

2. The colonists had no one in the British government to buy for them.

3. The British sent the Tea Act.

4. Some angry colonists drank all the tea in Boston Harbor.

5. Other colonies felt angry for and helped the Bostonians.

6. Thirty colonies united against the British.

DISCUSSION

Discuss the answers to the questions with your classmates.
1. Why were the colonists so angry?
2. What mistake did the British king make?
3. What famous revolutions can you name?

Write four sentences about an event in history.

> **EXAMPLE:**
>
> In December 1773, American colonists threw all the East India Company's tea into Boston Harbor. They were angry because they had to pay taxes but had no one to speak for them in the British Government. The British king closed Boston Harbor and sent 4,000 soldiers. Thirteen colonies united to help the Bostonians fight against the British.

DID YOU KNOW . . . ?

The colonists threw 90,000 pounds of tea into the sea. It was worth the equivalent of more than $1 million today.

July 4th

PREREADING

Answer the questions.

1. What do you see in the picture?
2. What U.S. holidays do you know about?

July 4th

July 4th is the birthday of the United States. It is a **national** holiday. Another name for July 4th is **Independence** Day. Americans celebrate July 4th as Independence Day because on July 4, 1776, the original thirteen colonies declared their independence from England.

Before 1776, the King of England **ruled** the thirteen colonies in America. The colonists were angry with the King because he made them pay taxes. They wanted their independence from England. A war started in 1775 between the colonists and soldiers from England. The colonists won the war. They wanted to say why they wanted their independence or **freedom** from England. So they chose Thomas Jefferson to write the Declaration of Independence.

On July 4, 1776, the leaders of the colonies signed the Declaration of Independence in Philadelphia, Pennsylvania. It said that all people were **equal** and had the right to live in freedom. A new nation was born. People rang bells and **fired** guns for the birth of the United States of America.

Today, there are many different ways to celebrate July 4th. During the day, many people get together with friends and family members for **picnics**. Many cities have **parades** with bands in the streets. At night there are noisy fireworks. These beautiful fireworks of different colors light up the sky all across the country.

VOCABULARY

 MEANING

Complete the sentences with words from the box.

national	ruled	equal	picnic
independence	freedom	fired	parade

1. A group of people walking together to celebrate something is a
   _____.

2. A person or government who had power over others _____
   them.

3. Someone who shot a gun _____ it.

4. An informal meal that people usually eat outdoors is a
   _____.

5. If people in a place can do what they want to and live the way they
   choose, they have _____.

6. A special day that people celebrate all over a country is a
   _____ holiday.

7. When people in a country are free to rule themselves, they have their
   _____.

8. When two or more people or things are the same, they are
   _____.

 USE

Work with a partner to answer the questions. Use complete sentences.

1. What does your family eat at a *picnic*?
2. What things do we call *national*?
3. Why is *freedom* important?
4. When did your country get its *independence*?
5. Do you believe all people are *equal*? Why?
6. Who *ruled* your country 100 years ago?

COMPREHENSION

 LOOKING FOR MAIN IDEAS

Circle the letter of the best answer.

1. July 4th is _____ .
   a. the King of England's birthday
   b. Independence Day in the United States
   c. a national holiday in every country
2. On July 4, 1776, _____ .
   a. the leaders of the thirteen colonies signed the Declaration of Independence
   b. the English won the war
   c. Thomas Jefferson was born
3. Today, on July 4th there are _____ .
   a. many ways that people celebrate
   b. wars in many cities
   c. colonists in the streets

 LOOKING FOR DETAILS

One **word in each sentence is** *not* **correct. Cross out the word and write the correct answer above it.**

1. The Queen of England ruled the thirteen colonies in America.

2. A war started between the colonists and leaders from England.

3. Thomas King wrote the Declaration of Independence.

4. People fired bells for the birth of the United States.

5. Today, on July 4th, friends and family get together for kings.

6. At night, fireworks light up the sky all across the state.

DISCUSSION

Discuss the answers to the questions with your classmates.

1. What is your favorite national holiday? How do people celebrate it?
2. For what reasons do countries have national holidays?
3. If you could invent a national holiday, what would it be for and how would people celebrate it?

WRITING

Write four sentences about a special day.

EXAMPLE:

March 10th is my special day. It is the day I came to the United States.

I got off the plane, stood in line, and had my documents processed.

The Immigration Officer said, "Welcome to the United States."

_____

_____

_____

_____

DID YOU KNOW . . . ?

Americans eat about 150 million hot dogs on July 4th.

Helen Keller

PREREADING

Answer the questions.

1. Who is the person in the picture?
2. What is she famous for?
3. Do you know any deaf or blind people?

Helen Keller

Helen Keller was born in Alabama in 1880. When she was twenty months old, she got an **illness**. After her illness Helen could not hear or see. She was **deaf*** and blind. Helen was a difficult child. Her parents did not know what to do.

Finally, when Helen was seven years old, her parents got her a special teacher. Her name was Miss Anne Sullivan. Miss Sullivan worked with Helen every day. She took Helen's hand and spelled a word in her hand. Helen soon learned to say what she wanted in this way.

In 1900, Helen entered Radcliffe College. Miss Sullivan sat next to Helen in class. She spelled all the words into Helen's hand. Miss Sullivan also read to Helen **constantly**. At that time there were only a few books for the blind. These were **braille** books. They had an alphabet made with dots that blind people could read with their fingers. Helen **graduated** from Radcliffe with **honors**.

Helen wrote books like *The Story of My Life* and *Midstream—My Later Life*. She also wrote magazine **articles** and spoke all over the country. She learned to speak. It was not easy to understand her. Miss Sullivan **repeated** what Helen said. Helen spoke about the deaf and the blind. People everywhere became interested. There was new hope for the deaf and the blind.

*people often say *hearing impaired* for deaf

VOCABULARY

 **MEANING**

Complete the sentences with words from the box.

illness	constantly	graduated	articles
deaf	braille	honors	repeated

1. A person who does something _____ does it all the time.
2. The special alphabet made with dots for people who cannot see is _____ .
3. Pieces of writing in newspapers or magazines are _____ .
4. A person who cannot hear is _____ .
5. When you completed your degree in a college or university, you _____ .
6. When you said something again, you _____ it.
7. A sickness or a disease is an _____ .
8. When a student is excellent in her studies, she graduates with _____ .

USE

Work with a partner to answer the questions. Use complete sentences.

1. How do *deaf* people communicate?
2. What else do we give *honors* for?
3. Why is it important to *graduate*?
4. What is the difference between an *illness* and a disability?
5. How does a *blind* person see?
6. What *articles* have you read this week?

COMPREHENSION

 LOOKING FOR MAIN IDEAS

Circle the letter of the best answer.

1. When Helen was a baby, she _____.
   a. became blind
   b. became deaf and blind
   c. could not hear

2. Helen had _____.
   a. a special teacher
   b. old parents
   c. one hand

3. Helen Keller _____.
   a. read only two books
   b. did not finish college
   c. graduated from college

 LOOKING FOR DETAILS

Number the sentences 1 through 8 to show the correct order.

____ She got a special teacher when she was seven.

____ In 1900, she entered Radcliffe College.

____ When she was twenty months old, she became deaf and blind.

____ Helen Keller was born in 1880.

____ Helen graduated from college with honors.

____ Helen spoke about the deaf and blind everywhere.

____ Her teacher's name was Anne Sullivan.

____ Miss Sullivan sat next to Helen in class and spelled the words in her hand.

DISCUSSION

Discuss the answers to the questions with your classmates.

1. What famous deaf or blind people do you know?
2. What are the problems when you are deaf and blind?
3. What do we do today to help people with disabilities?

WRITING

Write four sentences about someone who has an illness or a disability.

EXAMPLE:

The boxer Muhammad Ali was born in January 1942. He won an Olympic Gold medal, and he won the World Heavyweight Championship three times. He also won the Presidential Medal of Freedom in 2005. Sadly, he now has Parkinson's disease, but he still works with the United Nations.

DID YOU KNOW . . . ?

Helen Keller was a student of Alexander Graham Bell, the inventor of the telephone. They were good friends.

New York City

PREREADING

Answer the questions.

1. What do you see in the picture?

2. What do you know about New York City?

New York City

New York City is the largest city in the United States. More than 8 million people live there. New York has very tall buildings like the Chrysler Building and the Empire State Building. It is the biggest **port** in the world. Thousands of ships come to the port of New York each year. It has Macy's, one of the biggest stores in the world. New York also has the largest lady in the world—the Statue of Liberty.

New York is a very **cosmopolitan** city. People from many countries come to live in New York. Three quarters, or 75 percent, of the people in New York City come from five groups: African American, Jewish, Italian, Puerto Rican, and Irish. The other **quarter**, or 25 percent, comes from all over the world.

New York City is the center for culture in the United States. It has the **finest museums** and best art **galleries** in the country. If you want to see a **play**, there are many theaters you can go to on Broadway. The street called Broadway is the center for theater in the United States.

People call New York City the "Big Apple." **Jazz** musicians in the 1920s gave New York this name. When a musician says he is going to the Big Apple, it means he is the best. Today, New York is still the U.S. center for art and business.

VOCABULARY

 MEANING

Complete the sentences with words from the box.

port	quarter	museums	play
cosmopolitan	finest	galleries	jazz

1. Places where people go to see paintings are _____.

2. A city where there are people from different parts of the world is _____.

3. _____ is a popular kind of music that began in the 1920s.

4. A town with a harbor where ships can stop is a _____.

5. When something is cut into four parts, each part is a _____.

6. If something is the _____, it is the best quality.

7. _____ are buildings where people go to see important things from science, art, or history.

8. A performance in a theater is called a _____.

 USE

Work with a partner to answer the questions. Use complete sentences.

1. Which is better, a film or a *play*? Why?
2. Who is your favorite *jazz* musician?
3. How many U.S. *ports* can you name?
4. What is the *cosmopolitan* mix where you are?
5. What is the *finest* painting you know?
6. What are some famous *galleries* in your country?

COMPREHENSION

LOOKING FOR MAIN IDEAS

Circle the letter of the best answer.

1. New York _____ .
   a. has the largest ladies in the United States
   b. is the largest city in the United States
   c. is a tall city

2. New York is _____ .
   a. an African American and Irish city
   b. a cosmopolitan city
   c. three quarters Puerto Rican

3. New York _____ .
   a. has all of its galleries on Broadway
   b. has only museums
   c. is the center for culture in the United States

LOOKING FOR DETAILS

One **word or number in each sentence is** *not* **correct. Cross it out and write the correct answer above it.**

1. More than 11 million people live in New York City.

2. Three quarters of the people in New York come from four groups.

3. The street called Liberty is the center for theater.

4. Jazz musicians in the 1960s called New York the "Big Apple."

5. Macy's is one of the biggest ships in New York.

6. Thousands of plays come to the port of New York each year.

DISCUSSION

Discuss the answers to the questions with your classmates.

1. Which is your favorite big city? Describe it.
2. Do you like to live in a big city? Why?
3. What is your favorite museum? Why?

WRITING

Write four sentences about your favorite painting.

EXAMPLE:

The finest painting I know is the Mona Lisa. Leonardo da Vinci painted it.

When you look at it, it is very small. The little smile on the woman's face is

what I like best.

DID YOU KNOW . . . ?
New York City has the most skyscrapers in the world.

The Story of Ben and Jerry's

PREREADING

Answer the questions.

1. Who is in the picture?
2. Why are they famous?

The Story of Ben and Jerry's

Ben Cohen and Jerry Greenfield were **childhood** friends. In 1978, they decided to start an ice cream business. They took a $5 course on how to make ice cream. Then they opened an ice cream store in Burlington, Vermont.

They wanted their ice cream to be special. They used fresh milk and cream from Vermont family farms and lots of natural ingredients. They added big pieces of fruit, cookies, chocolate, and nuts to make unusual **flavors**. They wanted people to try their ice cream, so they gave out free **samples** all the time. The first year they didn't **make a profit**. Four years later, they had a business worth over $2 million.

Ben and Jerry were not **typical** businessmen. They didn't want Ben and Jerry's to be like other big businesses. They wanted to help people who needed it. They started the Ben and Jerry's **Foundation**. The foundation gave 7.5 percent of the company's profit to **charities**. They bought their **ingredients** from companies that helped the poor. Ben and Jerry's often gave free ice cream to charity events in Vermont. Every Ben and Jerry's Ice Cream Factory worker got 3 pints of free ice cream every day!

Ben and Jerry sold their company for $326 million in 2000. But Ben and Jerry's Foundation continues as before with the new owners.

VOCABULARY

 MEANING

Complete the sentences with words from the box.

childhood	samples	typical	charities
flavors	make a profit	foundation	ingredients

1. A private organization that gives money to help people is a

   _____.

2. Your _____ is the time in your life when you were a child.

 UNIT 22

3. In business, companies _____ if they take in more money than they spend.

4. _____ are the foods you put together to make something, like pizza.

5. Something that is _____ is like most other things of its kind.

6. Organizations that get money from people and give it to people in need are _____.

7. _____ are what you taste when you put food or drink in your mouth.

8. _____ are what companies give customers, to help them decide if they want to buy.

⭐ USE

Work with a partner to answer the questions. Use complete sentences.

1. What was your favorite thing to do during your *childhood*?
2. What are the *ingredients* of your favorite dish?
3. What *samples* have helped you decide to buy something?
4. If you buy something for $100 and sell it for $250, how much *profit* do you make?
5. What is a *typical* day for you?
6. What is your favorite ice cream *flavor*?

COMPREHENSION

⭐ LOOKING FOR MAIN IDEAS

Circle the letter of the best answer.

1. Ben and Jerry were childhood friends who started _____.
   a. a charity
   b. special ice creams
   c. an ice cream business

2. They made their ice creams _____ and special.

    a. different

    b. free

    c. typical

3. To help charities, they started _____.

    a. to give out free samples

    b. to use natural ingredients

    c. the Ben and Jerry's Foundation

⭐ LOOKING FOR DETAILS

Circle *T* if the sentence is true. Circle *F* if the sentence is false.

1. Ben and Jerry were childhood friends.	T	F
2. They were typical businessmen.	T	F
3. They gave some of their profit to charities.	T	F
4. They used fresh milk and cream from Vermont.	T	F
5. They used a lot of artificial ingredients.	T	F
6. They sold the company for $2,000.	T	F

DISCUSSION

Discuss the answers to the questions with your classmates.

1. Why do you think Ben and Jerry were successful?

2. What kinds of people do you think Ben and Jerry are?

3. What charities would you give money to?

WRITING

Write four sentences about your favorite ice cream.

My favorite ice cream is sardine and blueberry. It is very special. I like how the fruit tastes with the fish flavor. Not everyone likes it, but I don't know why.

_____

_____

_____

_____

DID YOU KNOW...?

There is a graveyard at the Ben and Jerry's Ice Cream factory in Vermont. In the graveyard there are gravestones. Each gravestone has the name of an ice cream flavor that didn't sell well, such as Miz Jelena's Sweet Potato Pie.

Thomas Alva Edison

PREREADING

Answer the questions.

1. Who is the man in the picture?
2. Where do you think he is?
3. What is he famous for?

Thomas Alva Edison

Thomas Alva Edison was born in 1847. He was sick a lot when he was young. Edison's mother taught him lessons at home, and he studied only the things he wanted to know. At age ten, he read his first science book. After he read the book, he built a **laboratory** in his house. Soon, Edison started to invent things. He was interested in the **telegraph** and electricity. At age twenty-three, he made a special telegraphic machine and sold it for a lot of money. With this money, he was free to invent all the time.

Edison started his own laboratory in Menlo Park, New Jersey. He **hired mechanics** and chemists to help him. He worked day and night. Once, he worked on forty-five inventions at the same time. Edison did not sleep very much, but he took **naps**. He often fell asleep with his clothes on. One day, he even fell asleep in a **closet**!

Did you know Edison invented wax paper, fire alarms, the battery, and motion pictures? But his favorite invention was the phonograph, or record player. He invented the phonograph in 1876. His other famous invention was the **lightbulb**. Edison died in 1931 at the age of eighty-four. He had over 1,300 inventions to his name! Many people say that Edison was a **genius**—one of the smartest people in the world!

VOCABULARY

⭐ **MEANING**

Complete the sentences with words from the box.

laboratory	hired	naps	lightbulb
telegraph	mechanics	closet	genius

1. A person who can imagine, create, and do more things faster than anyone is a _____ .

2. A special room in which scientists work is a _____ .

3. When a person sleeps for a short time every day, he takes _____ .

4. A place where people put their clothes is a _____ .

5. People who work on machines are _____ .

6. The glass object inside a lamp that produces light is a _____ .

7. The _____ is a system for sending messages over long distances.

8. If you employed someone to work in a job, you _____ that person.

⭐ **USE**

Work with a partner to answer the questions. Use complete sentences.

1. The *closet* is a place to put clothes. What are some other places to put clothes?

2. What other *geniuses* do you know?

3. Why do people *nap*?

4. How has the *telegraph* changed since Edison's time?

5. In addition to the *lightbulb,* what are some other things that make light?

6. What do you think it is like to work in a *laboratory*?

COMPREHENSION

 LOOKING FOR MAIN IDEAS

Circle the letter of the best answer.

1. When Edison was a boy, he _____.
   a. made a lot of money
   b. built a laboratory in his house
   c. invented motion pictures

2. In his laboratory in Menlo Park, Edison _____.
   a. worked day and night
   b. slept most of the time
   c. did not work

3. Edison invented _____.
   a. only a record player
   b. his name
   c. more than 1,300 things

⭐ **LOOKING FOR DETAILS**

Number the sentences 1 through 7 to show the correct order.

____ He died in 1931 at the age of eighty-four.

____ With this money he was able to invent all the time.

____ Edison was ten when he read his first science book.

____ In 1876, he invented the phonograph.

____ After that, he built a laboratory in his house.

____ When he was twenty-three, he made a lot of money.

____ He started his own laboratory in Menlo Park.

DISCUSSION

Discuss the answers to the questions with your classmates.

1. What other famous inventors or scientists do you know?

2. What invention(s) do you want to see in the future?

3. Who are people you know who do not sleep very much at night but take naps in the day?

WRITING

Write four sentences about an invention.

> **EXAMPLE:**
>
> The automobile is an invention that has changed the world. One hundred
> years ago everyone walked or rode horses. Today there are millions of cars
> on the planet. I hope they will be cleaner in the future.
>
> _____
>
> _____
>
> _____
>
> _____

DID YOU KNOW . . . ?
Thomas Edison was afraid of the dark.

UNIT 24

The Pentagon

PREREADING

Answer the questions.

1. How many sides does the building in the picture have?

2. Who do you think works in the building?

The Pentagon

The Pentagon is a building in Arlington, Virginia, near Washington, D.C. It has the offices of the U.S. Department of Defense. The Department of Defense **includes** the Army, **Navy**, Air Force, Marines, and Coast Guard.

The word *pentagon* comes from the Greek word *penta*, which means "five." A pentagon is a **figure** with five sides. Look at the picture. The Pentagon has five **rings**. The rings are inside each other. Each ring has five sides. How tall do you think the Pentagon is? The answer is easy. Each ring is five **stories** tall.

The Pentagon is the largest office building in the world. It has 17 miles of **halls**. People can **get lost** in the Pentagon, so the walls on each floor are a different color—brown, green, red, gray, and blue. This helps people to know where they are. There are also many maps in the halls!

The Pentagon is so big that it is like a city. Almost 30,000 people work there. The Pentagon has its own doctors, dentists, and nurses. It has its own banks and stores. It has a post office, a fire department, and a police department. It also has an important center for communications. This center **guards** the country. It is hundreds of feet under the ground. The Pentagon even has its own radio and TV stations.

VOCABULARY

 MEANING

Complete the sentences with words from the box.

includes	figure	stories	get lost
Navy	rings	halls	guards

1. A pentagon is a _____ with five sides.

2. Long corridors or passageways in a building are the _____.

3. If a building has five floors, it is five _____ high.

4. If you _____ , you don't know where you are or where to go.

5. The people who work on a country's military ships are in the

   _____ .

6. The five circles inside each other at the Pentagon are called

   _____ .

7. The Army protects a country. It _____ the country.

8. If a group _____ certain people or things, it has those people or things as one of its parts.

⭐ USE

Work with a partner to answer the questions. Use complete sentences.

1. What names for other *figures* do you know?
2. Who *guards* the people in a city?
3. What groups of people does your English class *include*?
4. When did you last *get lost*?
5. How long are the *halls* in this building?
6. How many *stories* are there in the tallest building in your city?

COMPREHENSION

⭐ LOOKING FOR MAIN IDEAS

Circle the letter of the best answer.

1. The Pentagon has the offices of _____ .
   a. the U.S. Department of Defense
   b. the Army
   c. the Navy and the Air Force
2. The Pentagon has five _____ .
   a. halls
   b. sides
   c. offices
3. The Pentagon _____ .
   a. has the longest halls in the world
   b. has walls of different colors on the same floor
   c. is the largest office building in the world

LOOKING FOR DETAILS

Circle *T* if the sentence is true. Circle *F* if the sentence is false.

1. The Pentagon is in Washington, D.C.   T   F
2. The Department of Defense includes the Army, Navy, Air Force, Marines, and Coast Guard.   T   F
3. The Greek word *penta* means "five."   T   F
4. The Pentagon has 70 miles of halls.   T   F
5. The colors of the walls are red and blue.   T   F
6. The Pentagon has its own police department.   T   F

DISCUSSION

Discuss the answers to the questions with your classmates.

1. What are the good and bad points of working in a big place such as the Pentagon?
2. What other government building in the United States can you name?
3. What will the soldier of the future look like? Describe his or her uniform and equipment.

WRITING

Write four sentences about a building.

> **EXAMPLE:**
>
> *Our sports stadium is a large oval. It has a running track around a football field. People use it all the time. I like to use it for power walking after class.*

_____

_____

_____

_____

DID YOU KNOW . . . ?

The Pentagon has twice as many bathrooms as necessary. When it was built in the 1940s, the state law required separate bathrooms for whites and blacks.

Arnold Schwarzenegger

PREREADING

Answer the questions.

1. Who is in the man in picture?
2. Why is he famous?

Arnold Schwarzenegger

Arnold Schwarzenegger's life is an American success story. It is about an immigrant who worked hard, came to the United States, and is now one of the most **recognizable** people in the world.

Arnold Schwarzenegger was born in 1947 in a small **village** near Graz, Austria. He started **weight lifting** at the age of fifteen. Over the next thirteen years, he won many **bodybuilding** competitions, including Mr. Universe and Mr. Olympia.

In 1970, Schwarzenegger acted in his first movie, *Hercules Goes to New York*. But he didn't become famous until 1982, when he **starred in** *Conan the Barbarian* and then *Terminator*. With these movies he became known as an action movie star. In 1991, he starred in his most successful film, *Terminator 2*. His **trademark** line from that movie is, "I'll be back."

Schwarzenegger didn't stop with bodybuilding and acting. He got a business degree from the University of Wisconsin and started to **invest his money**. He invested in real estate* and soon made a fortune. He married Maria Shriver, from the Kennedy family, in 1986. They have four children.

In 2003, he wanted to be governor of California. He won the election.** Arnold Schwarzenegger was a successful bodybuilder and movie actor. Now he is a politician. He is also **proof** that you don't have to speak English without an accent to become a very successful person in the United States.

* *real estate:* land and the buildings on it
***election:* a process in which a person is chosen by a vote

VOCABULARY

 **MEANING**

Complete the sentences with words from the box.

recognizable	weight lifting	starred in	invest (his) money
village	bodybuilding	trademark	proof

1. When something shows you something else is true, that is

   _____ .

2. As a top actor, Schwarzenegger _____ in many movies.

3. _____ is the sport of picking up heavy objects.

4. If you know someone is just by looking at him, that person is

   _____ .

5. Someone who put money into a business began to _____

   in it.

6. A group of houses, smaller than a town, is a _____ .

7. _____ is how weight lifters become stronger.

8. A name, sign, or word that makes someone or something recognizable

   is a _____ .

 **USE**

Work with a partner to answer the questions. Use complete sentences.

1. In what kind of business would you like to *invest* your *money*?
2. What are some *villages* in your country? Where are they?
3. What is the *proof* of success for you?
4. Who do you know who likes *bodybuilding*?
5. What is the name of a movie your favorite actor *starred in*?
6. What problems are there with *weight lifting*?

COMPREHENSION

 LOOKING FOR MAIN IDEAS

Circle the letter of the best answer.

1. Arnold Schwarzenegger is an American _____.
   a. immigrant
   b. action movie
   c. success story

2. He was a successful _____ and movie actor.
   a. village
   b. star
   c. bodybuilder

3. He became governor of _____.
   a. Wisconsin
   b. California
   c. Graz

 LOOKING FOR DETAILS

Circle *T* if the sentence is true. Circle *F* if the sentence is false.

1.	He started weight lifting in 1962.	T	F
2.	He won the Mr. Universe and Mr. Olympia competitions.	T	F
3.	He has a business degree from the University of California.	T	F
4.	He made a fortune in real estate.	T	F
5.	He is married with four children.	T	F
6.	He became governor of California.	T	F

DISCUSSION

Discuss the answers to the questions with your classmates.

1. What makes a great movie?
2. Do you think Schwarzenegger can become president of the United States? Why?
3. How will you make your fortune?

WRITING

Write four sentences about a success story.

EXAMPLE:

Jaime Escalante was a great teacher. He taught difficult students in Los Angeles. He respected the students and they respected him. Together they succeeded.

 DID YOU KNOW . . . ?

When he was twenty-one, Arnold was 6 feet 2 inches tall and weighed 250 pounds. He won seven Mr. Olympia titles before he retired from bodybuilding.

Hawaii

PREREADING

Answer the questions.

1. Where do you think the photo was taken?
2. What do you know about Hawaii?

Hawaii

Hawaii became the fiftieth state of the United States in 1959. There are 132 **islands** in the state of Hawaii. The **well-known** islands are Maui, Oahu, Kauai, and Hawaii Island, also called Big Island. Hawaii is about 2,000 miles from California in the Pacific Ocean.

The first people in Hawaii were from the Polynesian islands in the South Pacific. Later, people from China, Japan, Korea, the Philippines, the United States, and Europe came. Today, less than 1 **percent** of the people are pure* Hawaiian. Hawaii is **a blend of** many cultures.

Hawaiians believe their language is important. Hawaiian, along with English, is the official** language of the state. People in Hawaii say "Aloha" to everyone. This means *hello* or *good-bye* or *love* or *friendship*. They also say "mahalo" just as often as "thank you."

The Hawaiian Islands are really the tops of **volcanoes**. Mauna Loa and Kilauea are active volcanoes. They are on Hawaii Island and **erupt from time to time**. The **lava** from the volcanoes makes the ground rich. Sugar cane, pineapples, and beautiful tropical flowers grow there. The temperature on the flat lands is between 70 and 80 degrees Fahrenheit all year. This makes Hawaii a great place for vacations. Tourists come from all around the world, but especially from the United States and Japan. Hawaiians welcome tourists with leis*** of tropical flowers.

* *pure:* not mixed with anything
** *official:* as used by the government
*** *leis:* necklaces of flowers

VOCABULARY

⭐ MEANING

Complete the sentences with words from the box.

islands	percent	volcanoes	from time to time
well known	a blend of	erupt	lava

1. Mountains with an open top from which fire and smoke come are

   _____ .

2. _____ is the melted rock that comes out of volcanoes.

3. When volcanoes explode, they _____ .

4. An amount equal to a number divided into 100 equal parts is a

   _____ .

5. Something that does not happen frequently happens _____ .

6. _____ something is a mix of a number of things.

7. Someone or something that is famous is _____ .

8. _____ are lands with water all round them.

⭐ USE

Work with a partner to answer the questions. Use complete sentences.

1. For what *percent* of your day do you study English?
2. Why does a volcano *erupt*?
3. What restaurants do you like to visit *from time to time*?
4. What are some *well-known* islands you know about?
5. What countries do you know about that have *a blend of* different cultures?
6. What color is *lava* when it is hot, and what color is it when it is cold?

COMPREHENSION

 LOOKING FOR MAIN IDEAS

Circle the letter of the best answer.

1. Hawaii is a state that is _____.
   a. more than 100 islands
   b. one of the first states in the United States
   c. near California in the Atlantic Ocean
2. In Hawaii you will find _____.
   a. that people speak only English
   b. a blend of different cultures and languages
   c. many pure Hawaiians
3. Hawaii has _____.
   a. very cold weather in January
   b. no active volcanoes
   c. good land for growing fruit and flowers

 LOOKING FOR DETAILS

One **word in each sentence is** *not* **correct. Cross out the word and write the correct answer above it.**

1. There are 132 islands in the state of Hiawatha.

2. The flat islands are Maui, Oahu, Kauai, and Hawaii Island.

3. The first people in Hawaii were from the Poland islands.

4. Hawaii is a band of many cultures.

5. Sugar cake, pineapples, and beautiful flowers grow there.

6. The temperature is 70 to 80 degrees Celsius all year.

DISCUSSION

Discuss the answers to the questions with your classmates.

1. Why do you think people like to visit Hawaii?
2. What is the problem with volcanoes?
3. What is the advantage of volcanoes?

WRITING

Write four sentences about an island or group of islands you know about.

EXAMPLE:

The Canary Islands are a group of seven islands near the northwestern coast of Africa. The islands are in the Atlantic Ocean and belong to Spain. There are giant volcanoes and beautiful beaches in the Canary Islands. Many people visit them each year, and they say it is one place on earth where the weather is perfect.

DID YOU KNOW . . . ?

The earliest leis were made of feathers—poor birds!

Yellowstone National Park

PREREADING

Answer the questions.

1. What do you see in the picture?
2. Do you know a place like this?

Yellowstone National Park

A national park is a large piece of land. In the park animals are free to come and go. Trees and plants grow everywhere. People go to a national park to enjoy **nature**. Many people stay in **campgrounds** in national parks. They sleep in tents and cook their food over campfires. They also walk on **trails** or paths in the parks. On a **gate** at the entrance of Yellowstone, a sign says, "For the **Benefit** and Enjoyment of the People."

Yellowstone is the world's oldest national park. It became a national park in 1872. It is also the world's largest park. It **covers** parts of the states of Wyoming, Montana, and Idaho. Yellowstone is $2\frac{1}{2}$ times the size of the smallest state, Rhode Island.

Yellowstone is famous for its **geysers**. These holes in the ground shoot hot water into the air. There are about seventy geysers in the park. The most famous is Old Faithful. About every hour Old Faithful shoots hot water hundreds of feet into the air.

Two and a half million people visit this beautiful park each year. Park rangers give information to visitors. They also **take care of** the park. They tell visitors not to pick the flowers. They also tell them not to feed or hunt the animals.

VOCABULARY

⭐ MEANING

Complete the sentences with words from the box.

nature	trails	benefit	geysers
campgrounds	gate	covers	take care of

1. Something that is good for a person is a _____.
2. _____ are holes in the ground that shoot hot water in the air.
3. A _____ is an outside door.
4. If you make sure something stays in good condition, you _____ it.
5. An outdoor place in the world where plants and animals live is _____.
6. Places to walk in a park or forest are _____.
7. When a park includes an area of a city or a state, it _____ that area.
8. Outdoor places where people sleep in tents and cook over open fires are _____.

⭐ USE

Work with a partner to answer the questions. Use complete sentences.

1. How can people *take care of* a park?
2. Do you like to be out in *nature*? Why?
3. What other words do you know for *trail*?
4. Have you ever stayed in a *campground*? Where? When?
5. What are the *benefits* of national parks?
6. What do you think makes *geysers*?

COMPREHENSION

 LOOKING FOR MAIN IDEAS

Write complete answers to the questions.

1. Why do people go to national parks?

   _____

   _____

2. Why is Yellowstone famous?

   _____

   _____

3. What do the park rangers do?

   _____

   _____

 LOOKING FOR DETAILS

Circle the letter of the best answer.

1. Yellowstone covers parts of _____ .
   a. Wyoming and Montana
   b. Wyoming, Montana, and Idaho
   c. Wyoming, Montana, and Iowa
2. Yellowstone is $2\frac{1}{2}$ times the size of _____ .
   a. Montana
   b. Idaho
   c. Rhode Island
3. Yellowstone has about _____ geysers.
   a. seven
   b. twenty
   c. seventy
4. Geysers shoot hot water into the _____ .
   a. ground
   b. air
   c. holes

5. The most famous geyser is _____.

    a. Old Faithful

    b. Old Yellowstone

    c. Old Hundred

6. Park rangers give _____ to visitors.

    a. animals

    b. flowers

    c. information

DISCUSSION

Discuss the answers to the questions with your classmates.

1. Where do you prefer to go in your free time—to the mall, the mountains, or the beach? Why?

2. What kinds of parks do you know about?

3. Do you think national parks are a good idea? Why?

WRITING

Write four sentences about nature.

> **EXAMPLE:**
>
> *I love nature. I like to go walking in the park in the clean air. I enjoy the birds and the flowers. It makes me feel good to get out of the city from time to time.*

_____

_____

_____

_____

DID YOU KNOW . . . ?

Visitors who don't like camping can stay in one of nine hotels at Yellowstone National Park. There are also small cabins. In all, there are more than 2,000 rooms at the park.

The Stars and Stripes

PREREADING

Answer the questions.

1. How many stripes are there on the flag?
2. What do you think the stars are a symbol for?

The Stars and Stripes

Every country has its own flag. The "Stars and **Stripes**" is a **popular** name for the red, white, and blue **flag** of the United States. Another popular name is "The Star-Spangled Banner." This is also the name of the national **anthem** of the United States.

In 1776, when the thirteen colonies declared their independence from Great Britain, the United States was born. George Washington was the general of the American Army. He decided that his new country needed a flag. There is a story that General George Washington asked Betsy Ross to make that flag.

She used three colors: red, white, and blue. The color red was for **courage**, white was for **liberty**, and blue was for **justice**. She sewed thirteen red and white stripes and thirteen white stars in a circle on a blue square. The thirteen stars and stripes **stood for** the number of states at the beginning of the United States. On June 14, 1777, Congress voted for this flag to be the national flag.

Later, new states joined the United States. This was a problem for the flag. In 1818, Congress made another law about the flag. The thirteen stripes stayed the same, but for each new state a new star was added. Today, there are fifty stars on the flag. Hawaii was the last star added, in 1959.

VOCABULARY

 **MEANING**

Complete the sentences with words from the box.

stripes	flag	courage	justice
popular	anthem	liberty	stood for

1. A country's national song is its _____.
2. _____ are thick lines.
3. Something that was a symbol for another thing _____ it.
4. A _____ is a piece of fabric with colors and sometimes pictures on it; it is the symbol of a country.
5. _____ is a different word for freedom.
6. There is _____ when a legal system is fair and reasonable to the people.
7. When people are brave in times of danger, they have _____.
8. If something is _____, a lot of people like it or believe it.

 **USE**

Work with a partner to answer the questions. Use complete sentences.

1. What are the first words of a national *anthem* you know?
2. What does *liberty* mean to you?
3. What do the *stripes* on the United States Flag stand for?
4. What is "a buck" the *popular* name for?
5. What does the *flag* of another country you know about look like?
6. Why is *justice* important?

COMPREHENSION

 LOOKING FOR MAIN IDEAS

Write complete answers to the questions.

1. What do the colors of the flag of the United States stand for?

   _____

2. How many red and white stripes are there? Why?

   _____

3. How many stars are there on the flag today? Why?

   _____

 LOOKING FOR DETAILS

Circle *T* if the sentence is true. Circle *F* if the sentence is false.

1.	The United States was born in 1776.	T	F
2.	There were thirteen states in the beginning.	T	F
3.	In the beginning the flag had two colors.	T	F
4.	The color white is for courage.	T	F
5.	Each new state gets a new stripe.	T	F
6.	The last star added was for Hawaii.	T	F

DISCUSSION

Discuss the answers to the questions with your classmates.

1. What does your country's flag look like?
2. What do people use flags for?
3. If you could design a flag for your school, what would it look like? Why?

WRITING

Write four sentences about a flag.

EXAMPLE:

My football team has a flag. It is yellow with ten red circles. The yellow
stands for sunshine, and the red stands for the championships we have
won. Next year we want eleven circles on our flag!

_____

_____

_____

_____

DID YOU KNOW . . . ?

Francis Scott Key, who wrote the words to "The Star-Spangled Banner," was not
a songwriter—he was a lawyer!

ANSWER KEY

UNIT 1

VOCABULARY: MEANING

1. flat land   2. origin   3. climate
4. nation   5. symbol of   6. population
7. join   8. Identity

COMPREHENSION: LOOKING FOR MAIN IDEAS

1. b   2. a   3. c

LOOKING FOR DETAILS

1. mountain → flower
2. Hawaii → Alaska
3. people → names
4. Hawaii → Alaska
5. stripes → colors
6. states → cities

UNIT 2

PREREADING

1. buffalo
2. in North America
3. 2,000 pounds or more

VOCABULARY: MEANING

1. immigrants   2. Hunters
3. Leather   4. waste   5. A herd of
6. followed   7. center   8. all over

COMPREHENSION: LOOKING FOR MAIN IDEAS

1. Where did the buffalo live two hundred years ago?
2. Why did the Indians follow the buffalo?
3. Who killed the buffalo for their hides?
4. How many buffalo are there in America today?

LOOKING FOR DETAILS

1. T   2. F   3. F   4. T   5. T   6. F

UNIT 3

VOCABULARY: MEANING

1. ride horses   2. ranch   3. describe
4. produces   5. a mixture of
6. proud of   7. boots   8. Texans

COMPREHENSION: LOOKING FOR MAIN IDEAS

1. a   2. c   3. a

LOOKING FOR DETAILS

1. T   2. T   3. T   4. F   5. T   6. F

UNIT 4

PREREADING

1. Colonel Sanders
2. He is famous for creating Kentucky Fried Chicken.

VOCABULARY: MEANING

1. governor   2. customers   3. chain
4. recognize   5. fast food
6. honorary title   7. franchises
8. interstate highway

COMPREHENSION: LOOKING FOR MAIN IDEAS

1. b   2. c   3. a

LOOKING FOR DETAILS

1. suits → boxes   2. school → work
3. senator → governor
4. title → chicken   5. times → cents
6. chickens → franchises

UNIT 5

VOCABULARY: MEANING

1. term   2. limousine   3. citizen
4. serve   5. in fact   6. expenses
7. earn   8. take the first steps

COMPREHENSION: LOOKING FOR MAIN IDEAS

1. You must be a U.S.-born citizen, a U.S. resident for at least fourteen years, and thirty-five years old or older.
2. You can be president for as long as two terms (eight years).
3. Many different types of people—lawyers, soldiers, farmers, teachers, writers, businessmen, engineers, tailors, and actors—are presidents of the United States.

LOOKING FOR DETAILS

1. forty-five → thirty-five
2. work → live
3. eight → four
4. two → four
5. high school → college
6. businessman → head

UNIT 6

PREREADING

1. Martin Luther King Jr.
2. He led the civil rights movement and fought segregation.

VOCABULARY: MEANING

1. assassin   2. clergyman   3. Equality
4. went on marches   5. protest
6. public places   7. Violence
8. make peace

COMPREHENSION: LOOKING FOR MAIN IDEAS

1. a   2. a   3. c

LOOKING FOR DETAILS

1. F   2. T   3. F   4. T   5. F   6. T

UNIT 7

VOCABULARY: MEANING

1. international sport   2. scores
3. court   4. played the game
5. indoor   6. ladder
7. gym   8. team

COMPREHENSION: LOOKING FOR MAIN IDEAS

1. b   2. a   3. c

LOOKING FOR DETAILS

1. ten → nine
2. gym → soccer
3. American → Canadian
4. balls → baskets
5. first → shortest *or* great
6. climb → run

UNIT 8

PREREADING

1. Abraham Lincoln
2. He was the sixteenth president of the United States, and he led the North to victory in the Civil War.

VOCABULARY: MEANING

1. ambitious   2. honest   3. leader
4. supporter of   5. lawyer   6. shot
7. civil war   8. hardworking

COMPREHENSION: LOOKING FOR MAIN IDEAS

1. Everybody liked Abraham Lincoln because he was intelligent and hard-working.
2. Lincoln wanted to be good at everything he did. And he said he wanted to win the "race of life."
3. John Wilkes Booth was a supporter of the South.

LOOKING FOR DETAILS

1. F   2. T   3. F   3. T   5. T   6. F

UNIT 9

PREREADING

1. the Washington Monument, the Capitol, cherry blossoms, the White House
2. Washington, D.C.

VOCABULARY: MEANING

1. wide streets   2. cherry blossom time
3. capital of   4. business   5. Capitol
6. picked   7. district   8. tourism

COMPREHENSION: LOOKING FOR MAIN IDEAS

1. b   2. a   3. c

LOOKING FOR DETAILS

1. T   2. F   3. F   4. F   5. F   6. F

UNIT 10

VOCABULARY: MEANING

1. ghosts   2. scare   3. Masks
4. Skeletons   5. Saints   6. devil
7. play tricks   8. treat

COMPREHENSION: LOOKING FOR MAIN IDEAS

1. b   2. b   3. a

LOOKING FOR DETAILS

1. F   2. F   3. T   4. T   5. T   6. F

UNIT 11

VOCABULARY: MEANING

1. sign language   2. savages   3. tribe
4. reservations   5. belonged to
6. dark skin   7. customs   8. lost

COMPREHENSION: LOOKING FOR MAIN IDEAS

1. c   2. a   3. b

LOOKING FOR DETAILS

1. F   2. F   3. T   4. T   5. T   6. T

UNIT 12

PREREADING

1. east side
2. six

VOCABULARY: MEANING

1. explored   2. colonies   3. culture
4. pilgrims   5. revolution
6. literature   7. map   8. Englishman

COMPREHENSION: LOOKING FOR MAIN IDEAS

1. c   2. a   3. c

LOOKING FOR DETAILS

1. parts → states
2. half → third
3. revolution → history
4. explored → started
5. English → Englishman
6. picture → map

UNIT 13

PREREADING

1. Thomas Jefferson
2. He was the third president of the
   United States and the main author of the
   Declaration of Independence. He was also
   a musician, inventor, architect, lawyer,
   politician, and archaeologist.

VOCABULARY: MEANING

1. doubled   2. library   3. author
4. talents   5. retired   6. expedition
7. declaration   8. architect

COMPREHENSION: LOOKING FOR MAIN IDEAS

1. c   2. b   3. b

LOOKING FOR DETAILS

1. F   2. T   3. T   4. F   5. F   6. T

UNIT 14

PREREADING

1. Beverly Hills (Rodeo Drive)
2. Beverly Hills is home to many celebrities.

VOCABULARY: MEANING

1. public parking   2. Celebrities
3. attendant   4. Jewelry
5. sport stars   6. elegant
7. tennis courts   8. shopping streets

COMPREHENSION: LOOKING FOR MAIN IDEAS

1. b   2. c   3. a

LOOKING FOR DETAILS

1. stores → courts
2. sports → small
3. small → high
4. celebrity → attendant
5. 200,000 → 35,000
6. jewelry → maps

UNIT 15

PREREADING

1. Theodore Roosevelt
2. He was the twenty-sixth president of the United States.

VOCABULARY: MEANING

1. rancher   2. nickname   3. Asthma
4. energetic   5. explorer   6. to hunt
7. intelligent   8. Blind

COMPREHENSION: LOOKING FOR MAIN IDEAS

1. b   2. a   3. b

LOOKING FOR DETAILS

1. T   2. T   3. F   4. F   5. T   6. F

UNIT 16

PREREADING

1. Niagara Falls
2. Niagara Falls is on the border of the United States and Canada.

VOCABULARY: MEANING

1. tunnel   2. The border of
3. blindfolded   4. spectacular
5. stunts   6. fascinated
7. tightrope   8. mist

COMPREHENSION: LOOKING FOR MAIN IDEAS

1. c   2. c   3. c

LOOKING FOR DETAILS

1. F   2. T   3. F   4. F   5. T   6. T

UNIT 17

VOCABULARY: MEANING

1. secret   2. To escape   3. safe
4. slave   5. underground   6. masters
7. brave   8. property

COMPREHENSION: LOOKING FOR MAIN IDEAS

1. b   2. a   3. c

LOOKING FOR DETAILS

1. F   2. T   3. F   4. T   5. T   6. F

UNIT 18

VOCABULARY: MEANING

1. on board   2. dressed up
3. complained   4. act
5. colonists   6. pay taxes
7. felt sorry for   8. to obey

COMPREHENSION: LOOKING FOR MAIN IDEAS

1. c   2. b   3. c

LOOKING FOR DETAILS

1. governor → government
2. buy → speak
3. sent → passed
4. drank → threw out
5. angry → sorry
6. Thirty → Thirteen

UNIT 19

VOCABULARY: MEANING

1. parade   2. ruled   3. fired
4. picnic   5. freedom   6. national
7. independence   8. equal

COMPREHENSION: LOOKING FOR MAIN IDEAS

1. b   2. a   3. a

LOOKING FOR DETAILS

1. Queen → King
2. leaders → soldiers
3. King → Jefferson
4. bells → guns
5. kings → picnics
6. state → country

UNIT 20

PREREADING

1. Helen Keller
2. She was deaf and blind, but she learned to read, speak, and write, and she became an author and lecturer.

VOCABULARY: MEANING

1. constantly   2. braille   3. articles
4. deaf   5. graduated   6. repeated
7. illness   8. honors

COMPREHENSION: LOOKING FOR MAIN IDEAS

1. b   2. a   3. c

LOOKING FOR DETAILS

3, 6, 2, 1, 7, 8, 4, 5

UNIT 21

VOCABULARY: MEANING

1. galleries   2. cosmopolitan   3. Jazz
4. port   5. quarter   6. finest
7. Museums   8. play

COMPREHENSION: LOOKING FOR MAIN IDEAS

1. b   2. b   3. c

LOOKING FOR DETAILS

1. 11 → 8
2. four → five
3. Liberty → Broadway
4. 1960s → 1920s
5. ships → stores
6. plays → ships

UNIT 22

1. Ben Cohen and Jerry Greenfield
2. They created Ben and Jerry's Ice Cream.

VOCABULARY: MEANING

1. foundation   2. childhood
3. make a profit   4. Ingredients
5. typical   6. charities
7. Flavors   8. Samples

COMPREHENSION: LOOKING FOR MAIN IDEAS

1. c   2. a   3. c

LOOKING FOR DETAILS

1. T   2. F   3. T   4. T   5. F   6. F

UNIT 23

PREREADING

1. Thomas Alva Edison
2. He's in his lab.

3. Edison had over 1,300 inventions, including the phonograph and the lightbulb.

VOCABULARY: MEANING

1. genius   2. laboratory   3. naps
4. closet   5. mechanics   6. lightbulb
7. telegraph   8. hired

COMPREHENSION: LOOKING FOR MAIN IDEAS

1. b   2. a   3. c

LOOKING FOR DETAILS

7, 4, 1, 6, 2, 3, 5

UNIT 24

VOCABULARY: MEANING

1. figure   2. halls   3. stories
4. get lost   5. Navy   6. rings
7. guards   8. includes

COMPREHENSION: LOOKING FOR MAIN IDEAS

1. a   2. b   3. c

LOOKING FOR DETAILS

1. F   2. T   3. T   4. F   5. F   6. T

UNIT 25

PREREADING

1. Arnold Schwarzenegger
2. He has been a bodybuilder, an actor, and the governor of California.

VOCABULARY: MEANING

1. proof   2. starred in   3. weight lifting
4. recognizable   5. invest (his) money
6. village   7. Bodybuilding
8. trademark

COMPREHENSION: LOOKING FOR MAIN IDEAS

1. c   2. c   3. b

LOOKING FOR DETAILS

1. T   2. T   3. F   4. T   5. T   6. T

UNIT 26

Vocabulary: Meaning

1. volcanoes   2. Lava   3. erupt
4. percent   5. from time to time
6. A blend of   7. well known
8. Islands

Comprehension: Looking for Main Ideas

1. a   2. b   3. c

Looking for Details

1. Hiawatha → Hawaii
2. flat → well-known
3. Poland → Polynesian
4. band → blend
5. cake → cane
6. Celsius → Fahrenheit

UNIT 27

Vocabulary: Meaning

1. benefit   2. Geysers   3. gate
4. take care of   5. nature   6. trails
7. covers   8. campgrounds

Comprehension: Looking for Main Ideas

1. People go to national parks to enjoy
   nature.

2. Yellowstone is the world's oldest and
   largest national park.
3. Park rangers give information to visitors
   and take care of the park.

Looking for Details

1. b   2. c   3. c   4. b   5. a   6. c

UNIT 28

Vocabulary: Meaning

1. anthem   2. Stripes   3. stood for
4. flag   5. Liberty   6. justice
7. courage   8. popular

Comprehension: Looking for Main Ideas

1. The red stands for courage, the white for
   liberty, and the blue for justice.
2. There are thirteen red and white stripes.
   They stand for the first thirteen states.
3. There are fifty stars, one for each state.

Looking for Details

1. T   2. T   3. F   4. F   5. F   6. T

AUDIO CD TRACKING LIST

Track	Activity	Page
1	Audio Program Introduction	
2	**UNIT 1:** The Fifty States	2
3	**UNIT 2:** The Buffalo	6
4	**UNIT 3:** Texas	10
5	**UNIT 4:** The Story of Colonel Sanders	14
6	**UNIT 5:** The President of the United States	19
7	**UNIT 6:** Martin Luther King Jr.	24
8	**UNIT 7:** Basketball	28
9	**UNIT 8:** Abraham Lincoln	33
10	**UNIT 9:** Washington, D.C.	38
11	**UNIT 10:** Halloween	42
12	**UNIT 11:** Native Americans	46
13	**UNIT 12:** A First Look at New England	50
14	**UNIT 13:** Thomas Jefferson	55
15	**UNIT 14:** Beverly Hills	60
16	**UNIT 15:** Theodore Roosevelt	65
17	**UNIT 16:** Niagara Falls	70
18	**UNIT 17:** Harriet Tubman	75
19	**UNIT 18:** The Boston Tea Party	80
20	**UNIT 19:** July 4th	85
21	**UNIT 20:** Helen Keller	90
22	**UNIT 21:** New York City	95
23	**UNIT 22:** The Story of Ben and Jerry's	100
24	**UNIT 23:** Thomas Alva Edison	105
25	**UNIT 24:** The Pentagon	110
26	**UNIT 25:** Arnold Schwarzenegger	114
27	**UNIT 26:** Hawaii	119
28	**UNIT 27:** Yellowstone National Park	124
29	**UNIT 28:** The Stars and Stripes	129